A y ,g woman's memoir of life during the First World War

Ursula Bloom

This edition first published 2016 by Corazon Books
(Wyndham Media Ltd)
27, Old Gloucester Street, London WC1N 3AX

First published 1959

www.greatstorieswithheart.com

Publisher's note: As this novel was written, and takes place, many decades ago, occasionally terms of the times are used that would not be used today.

ISBN: 1909752274
ISBN-13: 978-1909752276

Other titles by Ursula Bloom
published by Corazon Books

Wonder Cruise (fiction)

Many more titles to be published soon.
Please visit www.ursulabloom.com
for news, updates and exclusives.

Foreword

I wish to thank for the courteous help given to me so willingly by Mr. Charles Eade; Mr. W. Law of the *East Essex Gazette*; The Imperial War Museum; Mr. McLarney of the Frinton-on-Sea Urban District Council; Mr. Cadness Page, Librarian at Harrods; Mr. P. E. Westley, who was a special constable in Walton-on-the-Naze all through those four years.

I should also like to mention the debt I owe to the late Mr. MacDonagh for his book, *Living in London during the Great War*.

Ursula Bloom

Author's Note

At the time of the Second World War people said to me, 'This will be the most ghastly thing that has ever happened.' I felt that I remembered an even worse time when we were so entirely unprepared for it, and so appalled by what came and by our incapacity to find swift victory. It was youth which fought that war, believing that in so doing it would finally crush any chance of future hostilities.

The memory of those four years has quietly slipped away, and much is forgotten. Today 1914-18 has become something of a period piece. Little more. That is perhaps why I wished to write autobiographically about it. I was one of the young people brought up in a sheltered life, suddenly jockeyed into chaos, and this is just the story of personal experiences during that time.

Ursula Bloom

CHAPTER 1

But Death replied, 'I choose him.' So he went.

SIEGFRIED SASSOON

It is difficult today to picture the 1910-14 period, for then it was a bigoted world, the era of the autocratic individual, when today it has become the age of the masses. Society was carefully sectioned, all part of the imperial honeycomb. We were sons and daughters of an empire which we believed to be impregnable, and perhaps it was going to be the greatest shock of all to discover that – like other empires – it could fall.

We were jauntily young, enjoying perhaps one of the most exciting periods of our history. Jazz had arrived. The 'Bunny Hug' was here. Mother thought it rather rude, my father thought it rather funny. We were all aware that the sublime era of the waltz was fading. Those wonder shows, *The Merry Widow*, *The Count of Luxemburg*, *The Waltz Dream*, and *The Dollar Princess*, were getting a trifle timeworn, and the two-step was wearing thin. 'Alexander's Rag-time Band' was the thrill of the hour and what a stimulation! If silly old Lord Roberts was going about the country launching the idea that Germany was laying in stock to go to war with us, we thought it was just because he was getting senile and amiably forgave the old fool!

None of us dreamt that the peacefulness of spring-sowing and autumn-reaping would fade for ever in the August of 1914, and from the ashes of our love for country there would rise no phoenix. We fondly believed peace at home to be our abiding happiness. Wars to date had in the memory of man been so conveniently far away that they had not distressed many of us overmuch. If Grandmamma complained that since the Boer War eggs had never come down properly in price (they should be twenty for a shilling, as any fool knew!), and it was preposterous to ask more than eightpence a pound for the best butter, that was just Grandmamma, and who cared?

It was still the era of the horse bus, and lean tired horses with all their ribs showing plodded the streets of London. The early motor-cars, still unreliable and dangerous (of course), had been replaced by better cars. The aeroplane had come, quite crazy, our parents insisted, and I had met Grahame-White and Gustav Hamel, who had offered to take me up in his plane. 'Only over my dead body,' said my mother, I think with wisdom.

We had had an inspiring coronation, and the Prince of Wales had been formally installed at Caernarvon Castle; now we all believed that he would settle down and marry the Kaiser's only daughter, so ensuring our future peace. Not that peace mattered so much, for, when we came to think about it, nobody could beat Britain.

In 1910 I had left the comfortable pastoral rectory near Stratford-on-Avon where I had been brought up, for my parents' marriage had broken. I had lived a sheltered life, properly chaperoned, was too young to be 'out', a highly important moment in every girl's life, and had been educated privately at home. In fact I had not been educated at all. Any money there was, and there was very little, for my father's stipend was £300 a year, had to be expended on the son, not the daughter. All the right kind of daughters married young, and this had been instilled in me as a duty. I wished to comply. Nothing would have enchanted me more than a pretty wedding, and a romantic young husband, preferably a duke. I wished to do the very best for my family, which I loved dearly, with the faithful rather pathetic loyalty of any nice young girl of that period.

My mother, myself, and my brother moved to St. Albans. We received a meagre allowance from my father of £120 a year, and although that was a period when living was cheap, and being parson's folk we were unaccustomed to luxury, the allowance was insufficient for our needs.

My mother had to undergo an operation for a malignant growth which we prayed would never return. We did not talk about it, because somehow we felt that silence would strengthen our defences. It was quite wrong to leave your husband in those days, so we were under a social stigma, for my father being a parson could do no wrong. Social laws were cast-iron. It was the era of church on Sundays, of lower and upper middle class, county and aristocracy, all in their correct niches. No tradesman could even by mistake come to the front door, but must go round to the back. He could never open a conversation (as myself today with royalty), and had he taken off his hat instead of pulling his forelock to my mother he would have been asked to send in his books and the profitable association between the families would have ceased.

In St. Albans need drove us hard. My frantic efforts to

write for magazines had met with no editorial encouragement, and I began to lose heart in that direction. I had contrived to get my brother into a bank by appealing to an influential friend who had done his best. After three months' probation my brother came home one evening looking dim, and with a present for Mother with which to bias her in his favour when he admitted that he had got the sack. He then went off on his own and apprenticed himself to an engineering firm (a tremendous loss of caste to professional people, and, what was considerably worse, he was to receive no salary for the first three years).

We had economized in every possible way, and there had now arrived the hour when automatically one said 'No, thank you' to second helpings (always offered, for that was the correct social rule), and carelessly overlooked putting butter on the bread.

To the outward world we pretended that we had means, for that was 'the thing'. Only the vulgar were hard, up, though even they seldom admitted to it. Gradually the strain on our petty resources was too much and as something had to be done, I was the one who did it.

I had already committed a sin, for I had become engaged to a good-looking sympathetically minded young man of twenty-three entirely against my mother's wishes. It had happened when both of us had gone to stay with my great-uncle at Heath Farm, after Mother had had her first big operation and I had been shattered by the dreadful truth of it. I was painfully aware that we lived under a cloud, for she had left my father, and I had few young friends, consorting only with old people. On this visit my cousin Harry insisted on taking me to a dance at St. Albans Town Hall. Mother said I was far too young to go, but my cousin persuaded her, and off we went together in a hired cab.

At the dance I had met Montie, who was good-looking, danced well, and flirted, something quite new to me and most inspiring, I thought. Naturally I had been lonely. I was sick for youth and privately believed that one had to marry any man who kissed one. Fascinated by his chat and his love-making, and by having someone in whom I could confide, I got engaged. By the time Mother came to I believed my future lay in Montie's hands.

He was quite a nice young man and worked in an architect's office in St. Peter's Street. His salary was a hundred and twenty a year, and as three of us at home were living on that, I thought I should find it quite simple to manage on it with only two.

Montie was connected with a cinema being built at the time to his design in Harpenden, and owned by a certain Mr. Clements. The cinema required a pianist at thirty shillings a week, and threepence off for the insurance stamp. I applied for the post, and with some regrets on the part of Mr. Clements, who however did not wish to fall out with the architect, I was accepted.

When I brought the news home to Mother I admit that it was with some trepidation, and I bought her a bottle of port – the ruby-red type at two and sixpence – with which to soften the blow.

I offered the port, then broke the news, and my mother was far more upset than I had anticipated, saying that it could only have been Montie who had thought of this, for I would never have done it. She was wrong there. I pointed out that when one's entire income is just over two pounds a week, and someone else can earn an additional thirty shillings, it *is* something. She wept.

'To think that we have come to this!' she wailed.

Of course she was right, and it hurt her, which was a tragedy. I was the young girl of the new age only wishing to defend my family and support them to the best of my untrained ability. I privately was delighted.

The hours were fatiguing. In pre-war days nobody had any compunction in overworking an employee. The continuous programme began at half past five, ending at ten-thirty. On matinee days it started at two-thirty. My hands felt like flat-irons at times, and the only possible refreshment had to be snatched from the piano top whilst still playing with the other hand.

I worked in that sour-smelling but lovable little cinema where the cottage piano was concealed from the stalls by ill-fitting plush curtains and stood so close to the screen that frequently I went dizzy from the proximity of the exaggerated picture. There was no possibility of escape, for only the National Anthem at half past ten could set me free.

Then when the chocolate tray had been checked (the booking-office takings had been sorted out earlier), Montie and I walked to Harpenden station where we had to wait an hour to catch the midnight train back to St. Albans. At eleven the bright lights were lowered, and in winter it was icily cold, for although lighting and firing were incredibly cheap, those were the days of rigorous thrift.

I developed acute anaemia. I lost the rosy peach colouring which had been mine, and turned pale. I also lost two stone in weight, though I had been plump as a partridge, but it was some consolation that I had the Directoire figure – much in fashion – and that a corselette skirt was no longer a trial to the midriff. Mother never saw it this way. Mothers don't.

Occasionally my father visited us, always with distress to me for I loved him and fretted when after he had gone. Mother wept her heart out and had to be consoled. To be torn between love for both parents and a deep desire to do one's best for either of them was agony. To help a delicate brother and to remain faithful to an engagement about which there was constant bickering were in themselves defeating. There were moments when I actually walked out of the house vowing that I would never return, but of course I did. It would have worried Mother too much if I hadn't, and in those days no girl purposefully worried her mother.

On occasional Sundays Montie and I went up to London in the afternoon to choose films for future programmes. *Sixty Years a Queen*, *Les Miserables*, *Quo Vadis?*, and anything with Ford Sterling in it. We would have tea at the Coventry Street Lyons', which opened at four o'clock, and we lined up for this, returning home at nine at night. Mother thought it quite wrong, yet wanted me to enjoy myself, and so was torn two ways.

The bands at Lyons' were thrilling. The metropolis was gay, the lights bright. If the hansom cab was dying out, the taxi was rapidly coming in, and one could kiss in a taxicab where the hansom had offered its own problems. There was a jovial thrill about Sunday night in London, the Cockneys being hilarious, the flower girls doing a brisk business, for it was still the right thing to buy your girl a corsage to wear. It was the provocative era of Gertie Millar, Lily Elsie, and the Dare Sisters. There was a vulgar little man called George Robey creeping to the fore, and considered by the young to be jolly amusing, though the old thought him quite shocking! All the girls were privately in love with Bertram Wallis, who had ousted poor Lewis Waller, who in his turn had succeeded Hayden Coffin.

Those were lovely years, and if my home life had been happier I should have adored them, but we were under our cloud, and even a small cloud was a disgrace in that era. Our big house had gone. It was a social crime not to have two servants (£8 a year), but we could not afford even a 'general', which in itself was a sign of defeat but not so awful as having a 'woman in'. People cut me because my mother had left my father and I felt dismally alone, yet there was of course nothing that I could do about it.

That was where I was when the war broke out.

The first sign of the coming war was recorded in the *Daily Mail* of June the 29th, 1914, when it gave details of the assassination of the Archduke Franz Ferdinand and his morganatic wife at Serajevo in the Balkans.

We had always been interested in the Archduke for it had been a debatable problem as to what he would do when the hour of his succession to the throne of Austria should arrive. The old Emperor could not be expected to last long. Franz Ferdinand had so far loyally abided by his marriage but he could hardly hope to put a morganatic wife on the throne, or make his son the heir. All this would be exciting, we thought, quite unaware that it would be long before Franz Ferdinand's accession that the excitement would begin.

The shot was fired on Sunday the 28th of June. To celebrate the anniversary of his marriage the Archduke and his wife drove from a nearby watering-place where they were staying and made a formal entry into Serajevo.

Although a bomb was thrown as they went, it was after the mayor's reception and on the return journey that the tragedy occurred. The driver of the royal car made a mistake, either inadvertently or on purpose, and took a turning which by misfortune led him into a blind alleyway. There Princip the assassin was waiting. He fired his revolver at short range at the Archduke, hit him, and turning sharply aimed again at the Military Governor, but missed. The actual shot had however been received by the noble Archduchess who, realizing what was happening, had flung herself in front of her husband to protect him with her own body.

The wretched pair were rushed to the Konak for

medical aid, but when they arrived there the Archduchess was already dead and the Archduke died but a few moments later.

We received the news fairly calmly. Fathers said, 'Dear me, dear me!' over the English breakfast table, and mothers pouring out tea at the other end said, 'Isn't it awful?' but that was about all the thought we gave it. European royal families were always filling the headlines this way. It had been only by extreme good fortune that the King and Queen of Spain had survived the bomb thrown at the coach on their wedding day in 1909; the King and the Crown Prince of Portugal had been assassinated when they sat in the same carriage driving through the streets of Lisbon; and the unhappy Empress of Austria had been shot when out walking. The idea that the reaction to this murder would lead Europe into anything more than a passing shock was overcome by the comforting, reassuring, 'Thank God that sort of thing couldn't happen here.'

There was a miserable funeral conducted during a terrible thunderstorm, a grim prediction of worse to follow, though nobody thought of it as that. We had always been so comfortably sure of our smug little island (naturally we did not think of it as that, for it would have been *lèse-majesté* or treachery), and nobody could lay a finger on us.

We read about it for we enjoyed sensationalism and the papers sold on it. It was very shocking, of course, but nothing to do with us, and at this moment England was in the holiday mood.

Where should we all go this year? Worthing was select, Margate was vulgar. The elite went to Freshwater in the Isle of Wight, but that was expensive. My family usually went to Great Yarmouth in spite of the commonness this entailed, but Norfolk was our home land, and other members of the family met there. It was also cheap, which was very important to us. There was a boarding establishment where men could stay for twelve-and-six a week (no lunch). Somebody had picked up fleas there (it was the cubicle system), but what were a few fleas when one saved so much money? Mother was the one who made the fuss, and as she didn't get the fleas, my brother and myself were amazed that she should be so upset.

We'd go to Yarmouth again.

On the twenty-third of July the *Daily Mail* published a headline which shocked some of the older people considerably, for Austria had presented an ultimatum to Servia. I read the Servian reply handed to the Austro-Hungarian Minister in Belgrade, treating it as good casual reading, and not bothering too much: 'We have accepted part of your demand. For the rest we rely on your loyalty and chivalry. We have always been satisfied with you.'

I thought it sounded dignified, not realizing that loyalty and chivalry were out of date, for the first threadiness had crept into the old school tie, though we did not know it.

There was a certain pleasurable excitement about the apprehension of our elders, who took it seriously. If something happened, then it happened, and it would be fun to get us all out of our rut. Perhaps the young always think that way.

It was reported that the Czar had sent word to the Kaiser *as a friend* begging him to 'stop the Allies from going too far'. The Kaiser insisted that he was being driven into a war which he had no wish to fight, and although Wilhelm II never alluded in so many words to his patience being exhausted, that was what it was.

On Sunday the 26th of July I was beginning to think about details of the holiday. It was the usual English

Sunday, I had been to church at St. Paul's in Fleetville, and now was starting to fill a trunk which would go off as luggage in advance. Mother was not too strong when it came to this sort of thing.

That very day the Fleet was assembled at Portland after the review at Spithead, and the man who eleven years later was destined to become my second husband, was a snottie serving in the *Hindustan* there. Young Gower Robinson wrote in his diary:

> *Portland. July 26th*, 1914
> Lie-in till 7. Divisions 9.30. Very busy so I couldn't go to church. We were going up North at 9.30 a.m. tomorrow, but owing to the Austro-Servian show we are staying at Portland till further orders.

All that week I was playing 'Oh, you Beautiful Doll' and 'The Wedding Glide' at the cinema, with very little idea of what might be going on and anyway thinking that a change could only be to the good. In the Gunroom of the *Hindustan* the snotties were throbbing with excitement because something was up. Whatever it was they wouldn't have missed it for the world. Was it war? Would they go into action? and if so, what fun!

> *Portland – Sea. July 29th*, 1914
> Got under way at 7 a.m. It was a very misty morning and we started off heading S.W. However when we got a bit out to sea, we turned right round and headed up the Channel. Nobody, not even the Captain, knows where we are going. All the forenoon and afternoon we have been preparing for action. Ammunition has been stacked up all round the guns, extra stanchions fitted up in places under the turrets, mess tables taken down to the bag flats. We have had orders

> to fuse all lyddite, but not to throw overboard any unnecessary stores. Found time in the dog watches to have a game of deck hockey. It is now midnight, and I have just spent three and a half hours in the main top at night defence. We made a dash through the Straits of Dover at full speed, with no lights burning. We had orders not to fire at any German ship unless fired on first.

The morning papers gave the news of the Fleet leaving Portland for a secret destination, and now the older folks were appalled. I and my brother thought it interesting.

'It's that awful Mr. Winston Churchill,' said Mother. 'Somebody ought to stop that silly young man, he does ridiculous things, and now anything may happen.'

The Kaiser had signed a decree to mobilize the German Army; our elders were apprehensive, but we found something which we thought much worse. Wilhelm had actually signed his decree on a table which was made from the wood of the *Victory*, Nelson's flagship! What an insult!

August dawned. In the *Daily Mail* good hotels at Brighton were advertising vacancies at thirty-one and six a week, or for the week-end twelve and six. The leading article mentioned: 'Yesterday for the first time in its history the London Stock Exchange did not open.'

By the next morning German troops were in Luxemburg. I remember that I was far more interested in the enormous front page advertisement taking the whole page which urged me, 'Throw your powder-puff away, and use Papier Poudré, a triumph of toilet science.' No nice girl used make-up, though all girls wanted to do so. The advantage of Papier Poudré was that being in book form, with cunning little leaves of peach colour, your father was not suspicious, and your mother never gave it another look. To discreet maidenhood this was the last word!

It now seemed as if something was about to happen, which my brother and I thought was a good thing. It would be too bad if in the end the thrill of going to war was denied us.

The August Bank Holiday was approaching. Extra music had to be hired from the music shop on Hollywell Hill where every week I went and chose my pieces. We would on the Monday itself open at eleven in the morning, with the programme continuing until ten-thirty at night. On such days my mother came over and took an occasional picture for me to give me a rest, but it *was* hard work.

Mr. Clements the owner got fidgety and would come and talk through the fusty curtains while I was playing, which made things difficult. Some nasty old man had asked for '1812'. (I had to play any piece on request but one had hardly expected '1812' in the entire!) The usherettes, two of them, were worried over their holidays; could they get a long week-end, or not? That depended on Mr. Clements, for holidays were not smiled upon. When Mother came I went and sat with them just inside the door, and we discussed the holiday question, whilst *Who Will Marry Mary?* was being serialized on the screen. Mother had been instructed to start off with 'When we are Married', and instead, she had begun with the gavotte from *Mignon*, which Mr. Clements hated, and it gave me the jitters.

The audience were not helpful; it was the duty of the pianist to keep the audience under control, stop too much whistling by changing the tune, correct laughter in the wrong place, and level them up when one could. That night the moment that I played any patriotic tune they joined in with fervour, applauding overmuch, and whistling frantically. On the lamp-blacked slides latest news was scratched with one of my hairpins, and it was increasingly exciting. The night before a snottie whose name I did not know, and who did not interest me in the least, wrote this:

> *August the Third. Scapa Flow.*
> Turned up for physics at 6.30, but the P.T.I. didn't appear, so we all trooped down again. Nothing doing all day, so we found time in the dog watches for a game of deck hockey. Apparently Germany has declared war on France and Russia, so I should think it can't be very long before we declare war on Germany. However, we are all looking forward to a war, to give us the chance of wiping Germany off the map.

That was youth's angle. What fun this is going to be! My word, if I catch you bending!

CHAPTER 2

On Tuesday, August the fourth, when we were already halfway through the evening programme at the White Palace, Mr. Clements returned and started to talk again. He said that he wanted the national anthems of all countries who would be our allies to be played in a kind of *pot-pourri* at the end of the evening, ours as the final one.

I did not think it was a good idea. Already innumerable countries were involved, some with very long national anthems, and it would take a time to compose and to play, when all the audience asked was to be allowed to go home.

He looked at me with gaunt dark eyes on either side of a big nose which was like an eagle's beak. He was horribly worried, we knew that because his finger-nails were bitten to the quick (one of his nastier habits) and last week one of the girls had noticed that they were actually bleeding.

Mr. Clements was on the Stock Exchange (the cinema being merely a hobby), and with war coming he saw disaster ahead. It is pathetic that at the time I did not realize that his wife had a daughter by a previous marriage to a German, a girl born deaf and dumb, and both of them were in agony lest Olga would be taken from them and put into a detention camp. I had never heard of such a place.

Earlier this evening Brooker the commissionaire had gone. A policeman had come for him, which alone caused some perturbation, but he was an old soldier on the Reserve.

We wished him well, and those who could gave him something 'for luck', there seemed little time for goodbyes. This had brought the war considerably closer. Brooker, a very ordinary little man, who had never even been particularly brave with the drunks, suddenly glittered into something of a hero.

'God only knows what'll happen,' said Mr. Clements in anxiety. 'It'll be the end of the world as we know it. One thing is certain, England'll never be quite the same again.'

I was contemptuous. I thought he was cowardly, something to be despised in this moment of thrill. If we went to war (and oh, how I hoped we should!), England would rise with a glory never before achieved.

'Maybe it'll be nicer than you think?' I suggested as I wrestled with 'Poet and Peasant' on the cottage piano.

'You're just a silly little girl! You don't know a thing about it, and you'd better hold your tongue,' he snapped, then swept out through the curtains, which at the start had been second-hand, leaving me with a haze of their dust and facing the nastier bits of 'Poet and Peasant'.

The 'Pathé Gazette' flickered across the screen with pictures of the Reserves being called up, to be greeted with violent applause from the twopennies. A destroyer put out from Harwich harbour. A slide told the audience that so far – my tin clock told me it was nine o'clock, just before the 'big picture' – Germany had not replied to our ultimatum, and the twopennies booed.

The cinema darkened again, just above me lights played on to the screen, and the tin clock (one-and-sixpence) on the piano top began to tick away the last vital minutes of the old regime. At the dramatic moments of one's life one does not recognize the tensity of emotional crisis. Sitting there playing for Mary Pickford was just another night in my life. No more.

When the end came I played the national anthems, but the audience did not stay, for they were eager to rush out and hear if we were really at war or not. Not yet. I closed the piano lid, and pushed the borrowed music into a box, for at all costs we had to keep that clean or the shop on Hollywell Hill wouldn't take it back next Monday. I went through the deserted foyer, up shoddy stairs to where Teddy was waiting with his chocolate tray to get it checked. As nobody else came to do it, he and I achieved this together.

The two girl attendants pulled on coats which hung on a wall hook, the only attempt at a ladies' room that we had. There was no lavatory of any kind and in emergencies one had to go up to the station which was a considerable way off. Any natural need of this kind was vulgar and could not be mentioned. Mother always said it was better than in the eighties when one was prepared to die rather than admit that nature could no longer contain itself, and some people *had* died, she vowed.

I went downstairs again into the foyer which advertised next week's programme in big colourful posters to catch the eye. We should be running *Les Miserables*, a picture I had selected. Montie was waiting, in the green suit of the era, and with a stick.

'Have we gone to war?' I asked.

He didn't know.

It was a bright night as we locked the cinema doors, and walked to the station. Little prickles of stars were out, and the elm trees on Harpenden Common were like immense cardboard fountains for some stage setting. The gorse smelt of honey. We were exhausted, and I was hungry, but had bought a penny chocolate bar from Teddy and intended to make my supper off it.

It was eleven, and the day was over. The station lights were always lowered to save expense, and the place seemed to be half asleep. In the period of cheap living people encouraged far greater retrenchment than today, when nobody cares.

The unaired waiting-room was nothing short of a prison cell and we sank tired out on to the varnished form against the wall. The incandescent gas turned very low made a singing noise which became monotonous, but every night there was this tedious wait in a dimness like that of a vault.

My body ached, and although we talked as lovers do, of what we would do one day when we became rich, it never seemed realistic in this squalor, when what we most needed was sleep.

The old bent porter who walked like a crab, half dragging a leg behind him (souvenir of the Boer War), pulled a forelock at us. 'The line's busy tonight, ever so busy. Your train'll be late,' and he grinned. 'Blame Kaiser Bill, and that! They're moving the troops round all the time. I don't know where they're going, nobody does. But they're going all right.'

Montie thought that Mr. Clements must be in considerable difficulty, for, according to the newspapers, stocks and shares were making flying leaps downhill. The bank rate was bobbing about. (That conveyed nothing to me, I'd never even heard of the thing. Europe had panicked, said Montie.) Mr. Clements had never been over-popular with the cinema; a ready fault-finder he would lie in wait round corners to catch you out doing something you shouldn't, which had not made him liked. Montie had seen him go off on an early train which was unusual, for he usually stayed in the hope of catching somebody diddling him, but he had gone looking cadaverous as ever. 'He looked like an old man,' said Montie.

'But he *is* old, very old,' said I. 'Why, he must be forty.'

Train after train came through at speed, but all the blinds were drawn, so we could see nothing. For months we had sat there at this hour listening to the whining gas and waiting for our own slow train to arrive. Tonight that had changed. One after another, so close that it seemed likely they would collide, trains went through in sequence. It was very late when ours came.

It took only a few minutes to reach the Midland Station at St. Albans, generally almost deserted, though there they did not lower the lights as they did in Harpenden. Tonight the Midland Station hummed like a beehive.

We walked into the yard, up the wooden steps to the bridge top and on to the Granville Road, leaving the sinister outline of the prison behind us. Montie always saw me home, then we said good night outside the house which was at the corner of the Hatfield road, and he went on to his own home on Hollywell Hill. As we crossed the bridge, another train with drawn blinds shuddered through, shaking the earth on which we walked. The noise was accentuated by the lateness of the hour and my own fatigue, but it looked strange, for I was accustomed to trains which were a quivering ribbon of yellow windows, and the gloom of these seemed ominous.

By this time the Government must have arrived at some final decision, for it was well past midnight.

Perhaps we were at war! Had the first shot been fired? The fact that it might have killed somebody did not strike me at all. The lights of the city shimmered behind us, and glancing back we could see the square outline of the Abbey tower, resolute against the night sky. My wrists throbbed (they never stopped aching until next day), and I felt sick and ill, for I was working too hard, and eating too little.

We went round the high wooden fence of our corner garden into the Hatfield road. Even the little rowan tree in the front garden lost its scarlet fruit at night and turned drab, and I glanced up at the front bedroom where Mother slept, and where she always kept the light on for me until I returned. Tonight the room was unlit. There was no glimmer of gas in the hall bracket and instantly I knew that something must be wrong, for Mother and Joscelyn were not there.

'They're out,' I said.

'They couldn't be!'

They should have been in bed for some hours, and a flask of Ovaltine should have been waiting for me. Joscelyn started for the works at six, so could never stay up late, yet they were absent now. It was extraordinary that the face of the house should be dark at an hour when usually it welcomed me in the friendliest fashion. This was the moment when it seemed everything in my life changed.

I fitted my key into the door.

Opening it, the house conveyed the loneliness of one deserted. I sensed it as I crossed the threshold. Mother had always said that the dweller on the threshold whispered a warning (she was very 'fey'), certainly it happened that night.

I turned to Montie, always kind, always helpful, though frequently ineffectual. 'Don't leave me alone in the dark?' I begged.

'I'll stay till they come back from wherever it is they have gone. My word, I wonder what's happened to them?'

Horror came to me. It was a flicker of Victorian upbringing. My mother disliked and distrusted Montie and always had done; she resented our ever being together without a chaperone, yet here we were, in a completely empty house and *in the dark*. Such an idea was monstrous!

'We must light the gas,' I begged him. 'Have you a match?'

'Of course, dear.' He put down his stick (no man could be seen abroad without a stick in those days) and lit the match which quivered unpleasantly as he reached up to the hoop of peeling brass in which the burner hung. It did not light.

'The meter's run out,' he said.

The match died. I groped in my bag feeling the rim of every likely coin with my nail, and no shilling was there. I had the treasured half-sovereign wrapped in tissue paper for extra safety, waiting for the end of the week when I should be really hard-up. A florin, two sixpences, some coppers, and half a halfpenny which Richard Aldington and I had once split, each keeping a half. I expect his had been abandoned, but I was a most loyal girl, and nothing would have made me discard mine.

Helplessly I said: 'I haven't a shilling. Have you?'

I think Montie recognized my anxiety though I tried to conceal it. He knew as well as I did that Mother would hate this, and I was so scared that he would say something rude about her which I could not bear.

'I'm sure I have some money,' he said. 'Light another match for me,' and he pressed the little stiff box into my hand.

I lit the match and we peered at the coins lying in his palm. Instantly we knew the worst, for there was no shilling. Perversely the match flickered out again and we stood at the foot of thinly carpeted stairs which rose after an angle to four bedrooms above. I had forgotten the war. Being in the dark with Montie was far more ominous.

'What – what do we do?' I quavered at last.

I suppose he knew that I was torn between my inherent fear of the dark and the knowledge that to be discovered alone with him at this hour in the unlit house might be wicked. He took my arm.

'It's all right, dear. Nobody could possibly blame us. I can't think where they have gone at this time of night or what they are doing. If there is a fuss it's their fault for going. I don't see how your mother could be angry.'

If not angry, she would be hurt and disappointed in me. I was desperately fond of her and I did not want her to be hurt. The excitement of the war had been eclipsed by the agonizing horror of being in this position. We sat down on the lowest stair hand in hand. We did not talk, both of us were too embarrassed and anxious and I wanted to cry. If the lights of Europe were going out, far more urgent was the dominant fact that ours had already gone out and there was nothing we could do about it!

We heard the sound of approaching footsteps coming rapidly down the street to turn in at our front gate. I was thankful but apprehensive. There was the rattle of Joscelyn's key in the lock, by this time it must be almost half past twelve, then Mother came in. Montie called to her in case she should be alarmed, warning her that we were already there. When she spoke, I heard that her voice was distressingly tired, and it worried me lest she had overdone it.

'Jos and I went up to St. Peter's Street to see if we could hear the news when it came. We are at war.' She paused. 'Whatever are you two doing, sitting here alone in the dark?'

'The gas has given out, and we haven't got a shilling,' I told her; the truth sounded silly.

She said nothing.

I think now that the magnitude of the events of that night had affected her in a way that we three in our youthfulness could not understand. To her war looked so enormously final that by comparison with it nothing else mattered. She fumbled in her pock-marked half-crown bag, found the shilling that she kept in the centre compartment for this purpose, and handed it to Joscelyn. He took it to the cellar-head, rasping open the wheezy door, and instantly the smell of starved air came across the cheap little hall like a gust from some reopened vault. He groped in the dark against the meter, there was the tinny sound of a coin dropping, and Montie lit a match.

The light was sallow. It illuminated our faces which in the last few moments had grown jaded with fatigue. Mother was white, her cheeks seemed to be drawn in so that she looked quite different, and for a moment I wondered if that haunting malignancy was returning. At this moment, the actual beginning of the First World War, she looked considerably older than she had done before. I waited for reproof.

'We – we couldn't help it,' I began, almost in tears.

My mother's eyes had not given us even a second thought, I knew, it was not that which made her look so changed. She had been at school in Bonn in 1875, she knew more about the Germans than we did. She said: 'War will be so different today. I may not live to see the end of this, Heaven only knows how far it will spread, or even if we shall win it.'

It was shocking that Mother should ever think that we could lose! We were the greatest force in the world, this was the Land of Hope and Glory being made mightier still, and we knew it if she didn't. She horrified me.

Montie said: 'Oh, I say! Oh, my word! We've got Kitchener, Baden-Powell, and Jellicoe, how could we lose it? My word! What an idea!'

The light sharpened her weary face and she looked at us as if she were the only one who understood, which was annoying. The old always think they know, and never realize how foolish they are. Then she smiled at me.

'It's getting awfully late, you'd better go home now, Montie, and thank you for staying with Ursula. We must get to bed quickly, for Jos has to get to the works at six.'

Montie went to the door. It had always been a cheap door, the rent of the place was twenty-eight pounds a year and its stained-glass panels rattled when it was opened or shut.

He said, 'Good night, all,' and went out into the Hatfield road beyond. There came the distant sound of men singing 'Land of Hope and Glory'.

CHAPTER 3

After the cinema and the late night I did not wake until after nine. Lying there in the front room, Mother's bed in the far corner, mine under the window, I remembered that last night had been strangely different from its predecessors.

I looked out of the window. Was the day really changed? It was the same; hot and bright, fair with August. The milk cart was going the rounds, cloppety-clop; children were playing in the Clarence Park opposite; morning had begun.

I dressed and went downstairs where Mother was devouring the morning paper.

GREAT BRITAIN DECLARES
WAR ON GERMANY

was the headline, and under it:

ALL EYES ON THE NORTH SEA

The declaration of war, very much wanted by the

masses, had let loose the passionate tide of patriotism. We were in a state of excited joy. Already recruiting offices all over the country were clogged by eager young men who had gone straight from Buckingham Palace last night to help England in her need. When King George the Fifth and Queen Mary came on to the balcony, all the straw boaters in the world were flung into the air with enthusiasm. The sound of singing could be heard the other side of the Thames, some said at Clapham, where once the more seedy of my two grandmothers had lived.

To the manhood of our country England was now a maiden threatened with assault, and how they wanted to fight for her! It would be sheer hell if the war were over before they had the chance to get into it. Each at heart was a St. George, each faced the dragon individually and proudly. It was very thrilling.

We now knew that Sir John French would take control of the Army, Sir John Jellicoe of the Navy. The war would be over by Christmas, probably by Michaelmas Day, for undoubtedly Germany had never thought we should come into it and had been taken by surprise. Recruits were wanted, said the paper. *How* those recruits went along! They chuckled as they waited hours. They made rude remarks about Kaiser Bill. It was their war, said the youth of the country, and they were doing their bit.

As we read all this, Alfred Leete must have been preparing his famous poster *Your Country Needs You* from which the hypnotic eye of Kitchener fixed one and his finger austerely pointed to you yourself. Life was moving fast.

During that day we learnt that even the Boy Scouts had been ordered to report 'for war duties'. They were to act as a stop-gap for those suddenly joining the Forces, were to be helpful with traffic, and watch for anything suspicious. Even then the spy horror had become a complete obsession. It grew like a mushroom in our midst and for a time there was no ridding ourselves of it. The duties of the Boy Scouts lasted some weeks, they got Army rations and pay, and their parents were furious until the Special Reserve took over from them.

Next day there were astonishing photographs of recruiting queues, the young, the gallant, and the inspired. Joining-up seemed to provide a grand opportunity for having a good time. We visualized a khaki-clad Army dashing across to France and dealing such a blow that Germany never recovered from the shock. We'd march into Berlin. We foresaw a Christmas when a strengthened *Entente Cordiale* settled down to an eternal partnership with a great victory and the German nation ground under the heel.

'I only hope you're not misled,' said Mother. 'The German Army was always very powerful.'

When my brother returned from the works in his dirty blue overalls, Mother noticed that he had gone very quiet. She was one of those people who could read your thoughts, and she said: 'Whatever's happened, Jos? Don't let yourself be rushed into anything yet. You're under age, and you couldn't join up even if you wanted to. Think about it first, and when you do go, choose the regiment which is best for you.'

'Everybody's joining up,' he said sullenly.

He had always been one of those quiet people who are extremely obstinate, and when they go silent nothing will make them tell you what is on their minds. I had to start off for Harpenden, so I left them to settle the matter. I got my hat, a floppy one which all girls wore, over hair wrapped in a big plait round my head to make me look older. I deeply desired to look really grown-up.

It was striking me that this war might come very close to us, and although it was fearfully exciting, the first feeling of 'not quite so sure' began to jab at me. I had wanted a change, for my life had up to date been routine-ridden, and routine is something that I have always detested.

I had been very unhappy over my father's and mother's marriage breaking up, and my childishly stupid attempts to bring them together again having failed. I had always felt that I ought to have done that vague 'something more' which I had never achieved. I was haunted by the anguish that my mother's growth would return, and although I had tried to put that out of my mind, it was still there. Our financial difficulties, and the fact that insufficient meals did not buoy me up, made it worse. I was anxious about my engagement to Montie which had worried my mother so much although she had reluctantly agreed to it at the time, and I wanted to marry him, possibly because he was the only young man friend that I had. I knew that he was what was then known as 'beneath me', which in 1914 was a major obstacle.

Until we came to live at St. Albans I had not realized that his father had an open-fronted shop there, known as the Works, which had given me quite a different idea, and it was situated almost in the hallowed Close. He sold machinery, nails, hammers, kitchen equipment and such and had an unfortunate notice hung up acquainting the world with the fact that he also cleaned chimneys. When he met Mother, ill-advisedly but courteously he addressed her as 'ma'am'.

Facing family resentment, I had turned stubborn. I liked his old father and his mother had been kindness itself to me. Although I realized that these were not professional people I insisted on sticking by him. I stayed loyal.

Now a great outside event had occurred which might change everything, and none of us dreamt how much. We were well-coached imperialists, patriotism was a blazing trail, and such people could only see victory ahead. I felt that Sir Edward Grey had not been right last night when he had looked out of the windows of the Foreign Office across St. James's Park in its exquisite summer twilight, and said: 'The lamps are going out all over Europe. We shall not see them lit again in our lifetime.' When I came to think about it, far more important to me had been the fact that our gas had gone out, and I had been left alone with Montie unchaperoned at the wrong time of the day.

The morning's *Daily Mail* was looking to the North Sea. The Navy was out on business, and that was where the big coup would come, they foresaw. That very day a young snottie wrote in his diary:

> *Sea – Scapa Flow – Sea*
> We had to sleep in the Gunroom last night, as we expected an action during the night, in which case all the W/T doors down to the chest flat would have to be closed. Arrived back at Scapa at 6 a.m. and started to coal from a grain ship temporarily acting as a collier. Took in 950 tons at about 160 an hour. Nobody in this ship knows anything that is going on as the Skipper won't publish the news he gets.
>
> Declared war on Germany at midnight last night.

Young Gower Robinson was actually fighting on the war front, as I wrote fragments of scanty news scratched with hairpins on the slides when Mother came over to relieve me for a spell. Oh, how those slides were applauded by a war-hungry audience! Gower Robinson took it casually as he worked early and late in the Accountant branch of the Royal Navy, for he was a far less emotional person than I was. If he had had time to think about it at all, he probably would have said that it was a hell of a lot of fun!

That idea had already bogged down slightly on me.
By the next day life had changed very much, and the morning papers announced that the Germans had crossed the frontiers of France and Luxemburg; this made Mother glum.

'This is going to be a bad war,' she said, 'I am convinced of it.'

I had seen a gun-carriage going along the Hatfield road whilst I was dressing. My first gun-carriage was indeed something.

The papers had this notice:

> YOUR KING AND COUNTRY NEED YOU
>
> Will you answer your country's call?
>
> Every day is fraught with the gravest possibilities, and at this very moment the Empire is on the brink of the greatest war in the history of the world.
>
> In this crisis your country calls all her young unmarried men to rally round the Flag and enlist in the ranks of her Army.
>
> If every patriotic young man answers her call, England and her Empire will emerge stronger and more united than ever.
>
> JOIN THE ARMY TODAY!

It was to us a most inspiring message, moving myself and my brother, though my mother was far more impressed by a little advertisement she had found in a corner, and which was more after her own heart. It read:

> *Daily Mail* War Map on sale next Monday. Price 6d. Order at once.

'We could pin one up on the wall,' said Mother, 'and then they send you flags which you move every day.

Everybody ought to have one of these.'

When I got to the cinema by the routine train, neither Montie nor Mr. Clements was there. I checked Teddy's tray for him. Lovering, the operator, had questions he wanted to ask, but there was no one to give him instructions, so that I was shouldering quite a lot of responsibility for one so young, but the show had to go on. Brooker's dark coat with its gold lace rings round the cuff, hung pitifully on the hook, reminding me that we had no commissionaire. Would they expect me to help if we got a drunk in the fourpennies? Surely not!

The audience was scanty. Half the people had gone up to the station to watch troop trains going through, which was the right entertainment for a nice warm afternoon, and they had lost interest in Mary Pickford, Theda Bara, and Fatty Arbuckle.

We were thrilled with the news that H.M.S. *Amphion* had sunk the German minelayer *Königen Luise* in British waters. In wild elation I scratched it on the slide, and rushed to the piano, grabbing the keyboard from Mother waiting to greet the announcement with 'Rule, Britannia'. This was the way to win a war! The scanty house rose and cheered to a man! Hats shot into the air. God bless H.M.S. *Amphion,* already the war was almost won!

It made the next day more disastrous when I had to record on one of my beastly little slides that H.M.S. *Amphion* had struck a mine and had sunk with the loss of 131 men. Nobody quite understood how this could happen (in home waters too, who *had* let the cads in?). It brought us up with a jerk.

It was regrettably pitiful that in this moment we never gave a second thought for the men who had gone down in the *Königen Luise.* That was not our worry! We had got rid of them, and that was all that mattered.

I did not see Montie that evening until I had played

the National Anthem, and the audience had shuffled out. We finished the books and the tray, then locked the doors on the place, and started across the common to the station.

He began to talk. 'There's something I ought to tell you, dear. My word, I believe this war is more serious than we think, and every young man who can fight, should. If my King and Country want me, I'm going. In fact I *am* going.'

This day last week it couldn't have happened!

Now the war, only a few hours old, was sneaking into the private house. It was almost as if we – who had always been entirely free before – were like pieces on a chessboard waiting for some unseen hand to move us.

'It's all a chequerboard of nights and days, and Destiny with men for pieces plays,' I muttered.

'Whatever are you talking about, dear?'

'Just that,' I said. Somehow I had never thought of Montie as being a soldier.

He had been making enquiries and found that if he joined the Army they would give him twenty-four hours in which to put matters right at the cinema and with the office in St. Peter's Street. I could possibly work a little harder at the cinema whilst he was away – it couldn't be for long! – and I'd done quite a lot before now with the chocolate tray, the takings, and the slides.

'Yes, oh yes,' I agreed, then in a timid little voice: 'But where will you go?'

The right to the private life of an individual had never before been challenged in my simple existence, and I could not imagine what might happen next. I did not want him to go. I did not want him to be in danger. The Land of Hope and Glory was jolly fine in a song, thought I, but I did not want it butting into my own life.

He did not know where he would go, for the future of the world lay in the lap of the gods, and when you joined the Army they sent you where they liked, and that could easily be the last place to which you wished to go! In an excited voice he told me that he would be dispatched to train, and there was a sense of anticipation in his tone (it was a pleasurable anticipation) that suddenly conveyed to me the bewildering impression that men are born with the primitive desire to defend their rights and are not entirely anti-fighting, whilst to women it is agony.

'But you wouldn't go overseas?' I implored him. 'I mean, you couldn't kill people?'

'I shouldn't like it,' he admitted, 'but I might have to. I mean to say, if somebody started to whack at me, my word, I'd have to whack at him, shouldn't I?'

I loathed the idea. 'I'd run away,' I suggested with female discretion.

'They shoot people who run away. It's desertion.'

I liked that even less.

That was a depressing evening waiting at the station, and my head ached. I had always got a headache easily, but since last year a wonder had been invented in the form of a tablet (sixpence a bottle) and it was called Aspirin. It was a wonderful pain-reliever.

I kept trying to comfort myself with the assurance that anyway the war was bound to be over before the 'Terriers' could get through their training, though this did not intrigue Montie. He had got the urge; the tidal wave of patriotic fervour had stimulated every male in the country. He wanted to stand by a country which was no longer land and sea, but a woman in distress. A beautiful woman, and for that woman gallantry unbelievable was galvanized. This was the greatest thing that had ever happened! Already the Guards were in France, and the Royal Navy were on the High Seas, *and* winning.

The headlines in the morning papers had told us that loyal Liége had repulsed tremendous pressure by the invading hordes, though how she could hold on we could not imagine. The headlines were:

GERMAN DEFEAT BEFORE LIÉGE

HEROIC BELGIAN ONSLAUGHT

EVERY GERMAN WHO PASSED BETWEEN THE FORTS WAS KILLED

Every slide I had sent on to the screen that evening, showing that Liége was still holding on, sent a thrill through the audience. I remember that when she did fall, some days later, I did not have to scratch the slide, for I was at the piano at the time. I had no idea what music I could play for it. When the slide did come on, it was greeted by stony silence, and I began very softly as though out of the distance, ‘Through the Night of Doubt and Sorrow’. Mr. Clements had always been insistent that we must never play hymn tunes because it was sacrilege, but I felt there was nothing else I could play, and apparently I did the right thing, for one old gentleman was so impressed that he got Teddy to bring me round a big box of chocolates, which must have cost him a whole shilling!

Immediate censorship was established, because, so Montie told me, England was riddled with German spies, and they were simply everywhere. The spies had got to be weeded out, and if the Powers-that-be would not do it, then the populace would. Already spy fever was dangerous.

Our train came in very late indeed, and walking home everything was just the same. Same moon and stars, same sounds of night, same tiredness in my own body. Same good-night kiss in the shadow of the little rowan tree which never showed the scarlet of its fruit after dark. Yet already we ourselves were different. *We were at war.*

I went indoors, and the dining-room light was still on. Odd, I thought, and went to it; there was Joscelyn.

'Hello!' he said, then: 'I've joined up.'

When I could speak, I said, 'You're too young, and anyway you *did* promise Mother you wouldn't.'

He ignored that. 'There was a long queue. I thought they wouldn't have me after all the illnesses I've had, but they didn't bother too much. Most of us were under age, anyway.'

He was excited, and did not want to go to bed but wished to talk about it, for patriotism had got him too, as it had got at all indignant English manhood.

'Almost the only thing they asked me was whether I could ride. I've got twenty-four hours' leave to settle things, then I fetch my equipment.'

On the table lay his before-dawn breakfast, put there by my hard-worked mother. The platter waiting for the bread; the tea things, the tea in a Thermos; porridge, too. Joscelyn loved porridge and it took the edge off the appetite, which in our home was important. There was the jam dish I had known since childhood and foolishly loved; it had a ridiculous kingfisher on it. Here were all the associations with youth, strong firm bonds which I had thought inviolable, and the whole lot seemed to be breaking.

'Well, where is it all?' I asked. 'I mean where do you go?'

'It's the Herts. R.F.A. We shall be in camp in the Riding School up on the heath for a few days, then off we go to train; it's no good asking me that one, because the sergeant wouldn't say.'

I said 'Oh!'

'Spies,' said Joscelyn, 'apparently the place is busting with spies everywhere.'

I looked helplessly at him. Suddenly the infinite weariness of the cinema came over me. 'Oh, Jos, I am so tired, so horribly tired.'

'Well, there's nothing to stop you going to bed, is there?' he asked with brotherly candour.

I wanted to say something, the words I had always felt but which sisters don't say to their brothers.

I love you very much and I don't want you to be hurt. I don't want you to go away.

But I didn't say it. I went upstairs to bed, and I thought soon all the men would have gone, we'd be alone, rather helpless, very lost.

At the far end of the British Isles a young snottie who one day would be very closely connected with me, wrote this:

> *At Sea*
> Had the middle watch last night in the main top; packed up at 3 a.m. There was an awful spasm in the afternoon. One of the ships sighted a German submarine and we went to action stations, then night defence stations. We remained there for about an hour, but we weren't attacked, and we lost sight of them, so we secured. Deck hockey in the dog watches. I have the first watch tonight.

Mother was brave at breakfast and awfully proud that Joscelyn had joined up, but I could see that privately she was worried lest it would turn out to be a mistake. I told her that Montie would probably be in it today. Now it was just a competition as to when the men could get there.

London was getting down to sheer hard work. On the front page of the *Daily Mail* the Junior Army and Navy Stores (York House, 15 Regent Street) were advertising that they had revolvers, war kit, and Sam Browne belts for sale.

There was also one exciting bargain that took Mother's interest:

Sleeping Valise
Pillow
Bucket
Cork Mattress
Blanket and Bag
Complete £6. 0. 0.

She had already sent off for, and was eagerly awaiting the war map; she had decided that no patriot could live without this.

In London at this time there was a young man whose name was Arthur Denham-Cookes, whom I was destined to marry within a few months, though as yet we had never met.

He was the gay kind, half Irish, and with that lightly attractive accent ('Och, begorra, you'll be asking that of me, will you?'). He was a young man born with a silver spoon in his mouth, and a member of the Inner Temple. Here's a war, what fun, what fun! was his reaction.

His left hand was deformed from birth, and his great embarrassment was lest he would not be admitted into the Army with which his dead father had fought at the time of the Sikh campaign. At Umballa in 1846 George Denham-Cookes had entered a battle as an ensign and had come out of it a colonel. That was the sort of thing an intelligent boy could do in those days.

The Governor would like this one! thought Arthur, and he got the butler at No. 6 Prince's Gate to polish his late father's sword (hopelessly out of date) and informed his Victorian mamma that he was now about to join up with the Army.

His mother declared that if he did it would kill her; for a few hours they argued as they had done before, though never on quite so vital a subject, at the end of which time he managed to precipitate himself into the Territorial unit of the Irish Guards, for God, for King, and Country, and only the Irish Guards M.O. will ever know how!

I must say the young man had shot round London in a Daimler soliciting every bit of influence he could, and he had by birth a tremendous amount of influence; they must all have helped him.

When it became apparent that Arthur could not fulfil the essentials as laid down in *King's Regs.* (a handy little book which sooner or later most young people came to know well) he went on into the Royal West Surreys (the Queen's), and became aide-de-camp to an exacting old general (ex-Indian Army). The requirements for this appointment seemed to be a first-class Sunbeam car, a banking account which never became flustered, and cousins, uncles, and aunts liberally spattered about the peerage.

Arthur Denham-Cookes could supply all these highly desirable assistances to young gentlemen's promotion.

His mother had forty fits. His somewhat low-down lady friends encouraged him. Rigged out in faultless uniform ('I'm a nice little fellow when you get to know me!'), Arthur was a howling success.

In that hour recruiting stations were being so stormed that it is little wonder that they almost collapsed under it. Not to have fought in the war which would end all wars would be a disgrace, and each young man was a knight in armour.

'The Government has taken over the railways,' said Mother when I got down. 'I only hope that won't upset the holidays.'

'But surely they can't do that?'

'It's called commandeering.'

By lunch came the point which brought the war really home to us, for the ancient milkman arrived nearly in tears. Usually his cart clopped down the road where Dollie, the pony, ate our hedge whilst he delivered the milk.

He said: 'They stopped me at the corner of the road.

They took my Dollie out of the shafts! It's downright wicked! She's old, and she won't know what's happening to her. It'll be dreadful for Dollie.'

Poor Dollie had been commandeered!

I kept thinking about her as I walked to the cinema, I had the feeling that this war wasn't going the way we had expected. Anyway it was a man's war, not a woman's, and men seemed not to be so shocked at the thought of fighting as women were. It might be thrilling but already nasty things seemed to be happening. Dollie for instance, and even at that moment life moved too fast.

Montie arrived about nine o'clock, and he said: 'I'm a soldier now. Tomorrow night I shall be with the boys in the Riding School.'

I kept brave about it till we got to the lonely station that night, then I wept.

'My word, what a fuss you make!' said he. 'The war'll be over by Christmas if not before. Nowadays no war could last more than a few weeks, this one'll cost three million a day. Fancy that, now!'

At midnight we came for the last time to the little rowan tree in the garden, hands interlocked. In distress I said, 'What will I do tomorrow when I'm all alone?'

'You'll be all right. You'll do your bit.'

'I'll be thinking of you.'

'I'll come and see you when I get a chance, and I'll make a chance, you bet.'

We waited for a distressed moment, then the Abbey clock struck, a sound we heard only when the wind was the right way, and it always meant rain. For no reason at all, I said: 'Hark at that! It's going to rain.'

'So it is,' he said, and kissed me goodbye.

Saturday morning, the eighth, brought headlines which told us that already 25,000 Germans had been killed and wounded. That there was a request for an armistice at

Liége, still battling on. That the French Army were in Belgium, and they gave the list of H.M.S. *Amphion* survivors. A casualty list. Our first.

The leading article in the *Daily Mail* ended seriously with these words:

> Might may be on their side; right is surely on ours. The patriotic ardour which has carried the French into Mulhouse and which has stood so resolutely behind the brave defenders of Liége, will prove a doughty weapon in the hands of the British, and of all the other nations forced into war by the overweening arrogance of a single people.

Next night I was alone at the cinema, and scratching the slides telling of the weakening of Liége, and its courage in holding on. When I finished I went to the dismal wait at the station alone. Tiredness made me nervous of the lonely walk back past the ghostly prison. I always hated the dark and I was too young for this, and much too tired.

Joscelyn had left the works, and was with the Herts. R.F.A. in the Riding School where they lay on the floor (and said they never slept a wink). But that was looked upon at this hour to be every young man's duty.

When Joscelyn appeared next morning he looked different in an ill-fitting uniform, breeches and the puttees which he said were the devil to wind. The tunic bulged and was creased; it smelt of storage and was crossed by a peculiar contrivance to hold ammunition, called a bandolier. But the boots were the worst thing, and the spurs down-right dangerous, tripping him every time he came down-stairs. The sergeant assured him that he would get used to them, and all he could say was that so far he had not noticed that he was getting any wiser to them.

Apparently the food had been so bad that they could

not eat it, and those who did were sick all night, which had made the Riding School downright jolly! Washing in the open in a bucket of cold water which he had to fetch for himself was horrid. I was aghast that he should have to face such conditions, and – valiant in my affection for him – wanted to complain to somebody and get help, so that this outrage did not continue.

'Oh, for God's sake shut up!' said my brother.

He needed socks. He had come to the conclusion that the ones the benevolent Army supplied were knitted in tin and had served in the Crusades. I said I would knit all night. I thought I could complete a pair in thirty-six hours. I had not reckoned on the fact that when I went to buy the khaki wool it would be almost impossible to get. All the young gents in St. Albans were bothered about their socks, and a glorious army of their mothers and their sisters and their cousins and their aunts, were going from shop to shop to buy khaki wool. It was short. It had also gone up in price, which to me was a calamity.

I have never been easily deterred. I got the wool, and I knitted half that night, and Mother did the same thing.

I had concocted one of my more scatter-brained girlish plans; if I went to the Riding School at dawn, I could perhaps hand my personal breakfast to my brother, but Mother thought I was mad. She said that there were hundreds of other girls' brothers wanting breakfast, and I must learn that when any young man joined one of the Services he had to abide by their rules.

She was wiser than I was.

CHAPTER 4

The charwoman who came to us for an hour twice a week for one shilling, told us that two spies had been caught in St. Albans and were shot that morning behind the Riding School on the heath. 'And serve 'em right!' said she, for the spy bug was spreading. She told us with enthusiasm that her son said the Tower of London was so full of German spies that they could not accept any more prisoners for the present.

Hideous rumours of German atrocities in Belgium were everywhere. We wanted to know the truth from Joscelyn and Montie, for as they were in the Army they must know, but for twenty-four hours we saw neither of them, and when we did they said no spies had been shot near the Riding School. Lots of talk was going round.

Another story began. It was that we could not hope to get our Army to strategic positions in France as quickly as required (the Germans were advancing with horrifying speed and had now invaded Lorraine), so the Government had hatched a better plan. There had been good reasons for the darkened trains which had vibrated their noisy way through Harpenden station when I waited there at night. The Cossacks were going to their appointed places in France. They had been recognized by their fur caps and some had the snow of Siberia still on them! The Cossacks were the chaps to win this war in no time and by the sheer weight of numbers.

Suddenly there broke a deep-rooted anxiety about the fact that Germany was making a major attempt to prevent our food imports; with this came the staggering realization that our glorious island was not self-supporting. We, always so sure of being best in everything, had believed that it was. The Land of Hope and Glory was showing a chink in its armour. Although I had been living with starvation nudging my elbow more or less most of my life, my mother pointed out that when there was nothing for sale in the shops it was a much nastier story.

On the tenth of August I went out shopping and had trouble at the grocer's. Ever since Pheasant margarine had slipped a sample packet through our door we had used it and had given up butter. Margarine was fivepence a pound, an agreeable price, but on the tenth it had gone up to tenpence! Sugar at twopence had advanced to fourpence-halfpenny. Naturally I refused to buy it for I thought I was being swindled.

'There's going to be a shortage, miss, you should lay in something,' said the friendly grocer.

On his advice I took my savings book to the P.O. and drew out a pound on demand. With it I bought two 7 lb. jars of marmalade at two-and-three each, four sixpenny tins of the best salmon, and a few other little trifles. It was alarming when the evening paper defeated my triumph by announcing that the Government was going to take action against *food hoarders*!

'But it's our money? Surely we can buy for ourselves?' I said, wretchedly.

Mother explained that when the country was under

martial law, we could not. Even the buying of a tin of food from the grocer came under that law, and could present its own problems. I began to wish we had never started it. Everything in these few days had become so different that I was bewildered.

The changing pattern of our living, all of which we had never thought could possibly happen but which *had* happened, and at an alarming speed, was complex.

The British landing in France was complete by August the eighteenth, and had been done without a single casualty, which gave us a certain sense of pride. The Kaiser's heir was now reported to be seriously wounded and lying at Aix la Chapelle where it was said that the Kaiser was by his side. It gave us a sense of thrill to think that Little Willy had come to grief, for we had of course no idea that there was such a thing as propaganda. That word was not in our dictionaries.

It was at the same time alarming that the leading articles in the morning paper kept insisting 'We want more men'.

> This country calls them with no uncertain voice; they are Englishmen and we can trust them to answer her call.

It had been something in the nature of a horrid surprise to find that when the thousands of oh-so-willing young men enlisted, Lord Kitchener had ordered it to be 'for four years or the duration'. I told my brother that was bosh.

'Of course it is! No modern war could last for four years, I suppose he wants to be on the safe side and it doesn't mean a thing, so why worry?'

Those young men eagerly growing their first moustaches and only too anxious to fight, found the going pretty rough. Many of them died on Salisbury Plain where they were drilling with sticks for rifles, and insufficient kit. Too many had joined too quickly, and nothing was ready. Frequently rations did not turn up, and the authorities were puzzled as to what to do next, but the men wore their patriotic urge like some religious fervour and it carried them through. It was our war, and we would fight it. If somebody *had* caught us bending, what-ho when we got up again!

On August the ninth the King had published a message to the Army:

> You are leaving home to fight for the safety and honour of my Empire. Belgium, whose country we are pledged to defend, has been attacked, and France is about to be attacked by the same powerful foe.
>
> I have implicit confidence in you, my soldiers. Duty is your watchword, and I know your duty will be nobly done. I shall follow your every movement with deepest interest and mark with eager satisfaction your daily progress. Indeed your welfare will be never from my thoughts.
>
> I pray God to bless you and guard you and bring you back victorious.
>
> GEORGE R.I.

That was the hour when we felt that the King must have inspired his men, but it was not followed up by good news. Brussels was to fall on the very day that Pope Pius X died, August the twenty-first. The news in the papers was not convincing, there seemed to be something of a hitch, and what it could be we could not imagine. After all nobody could afford to attack *us*. If it came to kicking, we were the kickers.

Every morning in the *Daily Mail* we read George Curnock's despatches, and every time a picture of the French came on the screen at the White Palace, I played the 'Marseillaise' and everybody stood up to sing it.

Soldiers had begun to filter into the audience (admitted free), and old ladies, spotting them, sent for Teddy and paid for chocolates to be handed to them. One of the usherettes told me that a young man got so many that he intended to take them round to the local shop and make money on them by re-selling them.

'You see, in any case he doesn't eat chocolates,' she explained.

The cinema audiences filled up again, because after a time troop trains get boring. We gave them the latest news on the slides as we received it. Montie having gone, Mr. Clements and I managed together as best we could. I locked up the chocolates at night, checked them and gave them out when I arrived. I put the wages into envelopes and signed for them. I ordered the films in advance for the shows, and saw the bill-posters, which meant getting there by an earlier train. I received no higher pay for this, would not have dared to ask in case it meant the sack, and anyway would not have expected it.

It was now known as 'doing my bit'.

The Herts. R.F.A. left for some mysterious destination, where they would go into training. The rumour was that they would be going to the east of England, but so many rumours kept flying about one could never be sure, and it had come to the stage when one doubted everything. Now all men were in uniform, it was an indignity to be out of it, and the white feather enterprise had started, and bands of girls and old ladies gave youths in mufti (and that was a new name, to me anyway) white feathers to show they had no guts. There was one story going the rounds that a local Boer War V.C., quite young, was on leave, and went round in flannel bags to the shop for the papers. There an old lady presented him with a white feather for his pains!

Mother and I waited to wave the column goodbye as they marched past our house at the end of August. A naval victory in the North Sea had been reported, with two cruisers and two destroyers down, and a third cruiser sinking. We were said to have lost exactly nothing, which was something.

We had word that the column would be passing our house about nine o'clock in the morning, so I got up and there we were waiting under the rowan tree, where we were doomed to wait, until at one o'clock I had to go off to the cinema. By then both of us realized that something must have gone wrong. I never knew what it was until I got home after midnight, where Mother was sitting up in bed knitting socks for my brother, her face swollen with crying.

The column had not begun to pass the house until four in the afternoon, and the hitch had been due to the hold-up of rations. The men had been served with their breakfasts as usual, but being expected to be on the march at eight, no midday meal had been arranged and none ever appeared. The horses had caused the delay. Some had been commandeered from the racing stables of Mr. Joel who lived on the Harpenden road. Becoming unmanageable, they savaged a couple of men, one of whom died in the dust outside the Riding School, and the other man who had been taken to hospital was not expected to live. The horses had broken several arms and legs of the pals who went to their aid, and when they did not kick, they bit ferociously, determined to do the thing properly. They had then bucketed the bottoms out of a couple of gun-carriages.

The scenes which ensued had been something like a minor battle and many of the young gentlemen had turned queasy.

It was two o'clock when they started, unfed and faint from hunger and the shock of it all. When ultimately they came jangling down the Hatfield road, my mother saw Joscelyn sitting on a gun-carriage and looking like a ghost. ('Thank goodness he had a gun-carriage to sit on,' I commented.) Acting on the spur of the moment she flew back into the house, snatched up bread and any available food there was, and rushed into the street to run beside the gun-carriage and hand it over as she went. Fortunately she was an athletic woman, and when other women saw what she was doing they copied her. They had luck in this, for every little while the column had to halt because more men had fainted and had fallen as they went, so they had to pause, pick them up, and put them on to a gun-carriage. In the end it looked as if every gun-carriage had its own corpses.

'Montie?' I said. 'What about Montie?'

Mother had not thought about him, only about her own son, which I suppose was natural. The column had gone, and we were aghast, for somehow we had never thought that they would not be fed. We heard a week later that they were at Livermere, near Thetford, where they would spend the winter.

We were off to Yarmouth in September, and I was getting worn out with the work at the cinema and longing for the break.

The news was muddling. There was a lot of talk about the German giant howitzers and the atrocities, and although the newspapers assured us that life was still going on as usual and there was no need for alarm, in our hearts we *were* getting alarmed.

When were we going to start winning the war?

On August the thirty-first, the leading article in the *Daily Mail* was warning:

> The heroic British Expeditionary Force has been forced slowly back but it has covered itself with fresh glory. We know from Mr. Asquith's statement on Friday that last week it was attacked

> by a German force outnumbering it by odds of more than three to one …

But on September the second:

THE ALLIES FIGHTING EVERY YARD

PREPARING PARIS FOR DEFENCE

Undoubtedly something *had* gone wrong.

Meanwhile the first of the military aeroplanes had gone up into the sky, in truth their lives in their hands. They were not fitted with guns, but went up armed with pistols with which it was intended they should come close and take pot shots at the enemy. This was the way the Germans were flying over Belgium, and although of course nobody said a word about it, save Mother, who could *not* hold her tongue, the time would come when they flew over us also.

Two days before we took our scanty holiday (without pay) at Great Yarmouth, Lord Kitchener himself reviewed the troops at St. Albans in a field above Verulamium.

'We must go,' said Mother, who loved a jaunt of this kind. 'Whatever happens we could not possibly miss this, for he is the greatest man of our time, and this is the big chance to see him.'

So we went.

We felt a little annoyed with Lord Kitchener predicting that this would be a four-year war which everybody who knew was sure it could *not* be! Financially no country could stand such a drag on its resources and manpower for a day longer than three months. 1914 would see the end of it.

That was a hot fine day, and everybody had bought penny flags (made in Japan) to wave at Lord Kitchener; when he came along he looked considerably smaller than I had thought. It is true that he had the face of a sphinx, but if we had hoped that he would appear to be optimistic, how wrong we were! At that moment he seemed to be in the last stages of a grim despair.

Walking back Mother and I talked about it. We had some doubts which we felt to be shameful, but it all seemed rather peculiar that the Huns could be coming through Belgium and Northern France and so far our forces had apparently not been able to beat them back. Casualty lists had begun in the morning papers, they were longer than we had expected, and growing longer still.

'It'll settle,' said Mother, 'we shall win given a chance; we've just got to find our feet.'

I was not optimistic. We, the young, had been so sure. Was it that England was not as mighty as she thought she was?

I let myself into the house whilst Mother went round to the grocer's to buy an egg for my tea. A letter lay on the mat; it was from Montie at Livermere.

Since the column had marched away Montie had written to me twice a week. He objected to the R.F.A. as much as Joscelyn did, but said less, for all the young men who were not the white feather brand were determined to face hardship to win this war.

I had an ominous feeling about this letter as I sat down on our weary old sofa, which had outlived its usefulness before it ever came to us, and I read it with despair. Montie felt that our engagement had been in jeopardy for some time. He knew Mother disliked it, and did not suppose she would ever change her mind. He realized that because I loved her so much, it could only make for difficulties ahead, and he had had some time to think about it. Perhaps if the war had never come we might have continued, but we couldn't as things were.

Mother had always said this would happen. It made me little happier that it *was* happening. For a moment I did not know what to do, then, anxious for him, for he must have been horribly worried to write the letter, I scribbled a schoolgirlish note before Mother came back.

Dear Montie,
It's all right. I understand. But please write to me sometimes.

URSULA

'I've got the egg,' said Mother coming in.

I didn't want it.

I could not eat my tea and I got up. 'I'm catching an earlier train,' I told Mother, then from the doorway: 'Montie has broken off the engagement. Please let me go. I – I want it this way.'

She came out to the gate, I felt her watching me as I went up the Granville Road. I don't think I knew quite how I felt.

That evening, Teddy bringing me a bar of chocolate found me crying as I played 'Invitation to the Waltz'. He brought my favourite usherette, and perhaps she caught me off my guard, for I told her what had happened. Her argument was that she had never liked Montie anyway, and thought I was well out of it. With a war on there was opportunity for everyone, I might even get the chance to marry an officer, so why worry?

In a daze I checked the chocolates that night, locked up and walked alone to the station. The darkness had ceased to frighten me. I waited in that dark place, remembering the grey-blueness of his eyes, and the gentle way his hand had held mine. His kind moods (he was a very kind young man) and the way he had always given me lilies-of-the-valley when he had the money – very often he hadn't any money. I cried a little, all forlornly, like a lost child.

Later I let myself into my home, and tip-toed to the room. Mother was asleep, or I thought she was. By my bed was the Ovaltine, a little sponge cake of the kind I liked best, and a tiny bunch of roses. It was the contribution of the woman who understood me better than anybody else in the world, and now, trying not to cry and perhaps wake her, I realized how much I loved her. So very much.

CHAPTER 5

Brussels fell.

We had started on our holiday and had come to Great Yarmouth. The place was fairly empty, for the thought of the east coast where invasion could come (though of course it wouldn't), terrified most people. Originally in the Edwardian days when we had come here it had been to apartments, then 'the thing' for people like ourselves, for only the very rich went to hotels. We had stayed in rooms at the Wellington Pier end (the more select and at all costs one must be select!), and an old lady always kept the rooms, and saw after us. I remember all the landladies had beaded bodices, sparse hair, and absurd little caps perched on them (never washed), and smelt strongly of perspiration and of gin.

But by 1914 apartments were no longer correct, and although the private hotel was unborn, the boarding-house was *de rigeur.* All nice people went to boarding-houses. The rest of the family were staying in the house they had always gone to since the year dot. My great-aunt Sarah was a foxy old lady, and Uncle Alfred her husband (the nicest of them all) was not considered to be quite the thing because he had not been born a Bloom. Uncle Alfred had lived a half-way life, not admitted to the family sanctums save if they were in a tolerant mood, and never asked for advice. The elder son, my cousin Francis, a seven-month child, and even that story did not help him much because he arrived two months after the secret wedding which had sent the family into such a state of jitters, had been born a cripple. He was a J.P., supposed to be a genius. His sister, my cousin Maud, was a large creature with the worst taste in hats I have ever known, but a kind heart.

Others of the family who came to Yarmouth were my great-aunt Augusta Frederica, unhappily named after her godfather the royal Duke of Sussex, and my great-aunt Fenella from Woodbridge, a powerful hirsute creature, a Jacobite and a Rechabite and most alarming.

We stayed in a boarding-house near the Arcade; it had sep. tabs., drawing-room tea, and serviettes. That was the era when serviettes and napkins meant something very different.

They fed one well in spite of rising prices, and if the bedrooms were small and the landing tank was a bit noisy, one put up with it gladly, because the boarding-house was *it*. I played the piano in the evening for them, and the proprietress offered me a glass of stout for my pains. This horrified Mother. 'She has never tasted stout in her life,' said she, outraged.

'Time she started. She'll have to one day. They always give it to nursing mothers,' giggled the proprietress's husband, who, so the gossip of the boarding-house had it, was 'no good'.

We were staying there on the pruned savings of an entire year and it had come at a time when the war was in a bad patch. The burning of Louvain had upset Mother, who as a girl had known it. Then Brussels. On

September the eleventh the *Daily Mail* was melancholy.

THE GREAT RETREAT

> It is an amazing story which Sir John French has to tell in the great despatch, and it is told magnificently, with a soldier's restraint and simplicity. We doubt if any army in any war has ever achieved such a feat as the retreat in good order from Mons, before an enemy of this fighting quality, supported in the ratio of at least two to one.

There was great agitation on 'should the clergy fight?' and people were getting angry about it, just as angry as they were about their white feathers and their spies.

'I suppose we *shall* win the war?' I asked Francis. It was the day my great-aunt Fenella was coming over from Woodbridge, bringing with her her rectorial husband Charlie Ratcliffe, looked upon by the family as yet another sop. The Blooms never took very kindly to husbands.

'Of course we shall win it,' he said.

'It would be awful if we lost.'

'But, Ursula, how *could* we lose?'

'No, of course not,' I said quickly, 'of course not.'

Field postcards from the front had come into being and were accepted with interest. ('Oh, have you had one of those too? I shall keep mine for ever as a memento.') Later they were detested for the very little news they supplied, and of course this applied also to the censored letters.

One afternoon I walked alone up the sand dunes which lie beyond Yarmouth to where the Yar flows out. I sat down by the river, still wretched about Montie, and there was no one I could tell, for the family would *not* have been sympathetic. A gunboat came from the harbour to the sea, moving faster than I had ever thought she could, and a bluejacket smiled and waved his hand. In but a few moments she was just a speck, then I saw a flash on the horizon and heard a dull deep report. A second gunboat came down the harbour to the sea, and later that evening we knew that the first one had been sunk with heavy casualties.

A deep feeling of disquiet came. We had retreated. Paris was threatened. Apparently tragedy had come to Mons where we had been going to win so great a victory. Mother and I had the good sense to realize that the one hope was that Joscelyn was safe where he was at Livermere. Montie was trying to become batman to an officer (this got a man out of gruelling route marches and other irksome duties), and Joscelyn, terrified of the horses which had been such a trial, was trying to get a job in the saddlers' shop with a sergeant friend called Harold, which would keep him agreeably in the background of the picture.

Those few days in Yarmouth helped us both, I think. The place had always been attractive, particularly the area round St. Nicholas's church. I had always heard that the organ had been washed up on the beach, though how that could have happened I cannot imagine. The 'rows' were wonderful; insanitary, of course, though nobody in those days complained; they were the width of a net, originally arranged that way with the intention of net-drying from house to house.

That was the time when villages and towns had a certain personality of their own which had been preserved. That area of Yarmouth was of the fisherman himself, with the market on the quay beyond, and the gateway to the Broads at the far end. Just as the sea end of the town was all entertainment, Britannia Pier ending Regent Road, with the Roman Catholic church half-way, where in my seedier grandmamma's lifetime, the waves had actually broken on the steps. But now the sea had receded so far that it was out of earshot. The shops which sold pink rock, dirty postcards, cheap flashy jewellery ('gems from the East'), were all jostled together in a rather ugly profusion. There were innumerable shops where postcard photographs were taken, or ladies told one's fortune for sixpence, the oriental flavour of the parlour being marred by the presence of blowsy seer and accompanying aspidistra!

It had all suffered a jar from the war and half the shops were already closing. It was now difficult to buy those delicious milk cheeses on their little straw mats, a Norfolk delicacy; the greengages were over, and the briny smell of bloater-curing was in the air.

'It's been a bad season,' said our proprietress at the last drawing-room tea, she in her best frock, and with seven-for-sixpence cakes, whole lettuces in case anyone wanted extra nourishment, and a glass bowl of shrimps. It seemed a peculiar drawing-room tea, but none of us went without, though I hated the shrimps. Francis, who was something of a tease, had told me of a sailor washed up dead, whose ears had been bitten off by shrimps, and I have never fancied them since.

As we got home, the Battle of the Aisne was beginning. The papers reported 'Allies' terrific shelling of the Germans on the hills', which was heartening. I had found an article on Twilight Sleep (just beginning to make itself known) in a paper which Mother did not know I had got, and I read it all the way home with great zest. The Battle of the Aisne was nothing compared with the entrancing article on Twilight Sleep.

Mother read Ward Price's dispatches, and was amused by the suggestion that young ladies with comfortable allowances should order parcels to be sent to the front, or articles of real interest to the soldiers. It was proposed that they should send:

Six pipes at 6d. each
Six threepenny boxes of Boracic Ointment for sore feet
Six tins of Vaseline to soften hard boots
½ lb. coarse cut tobacco
3 or 4 parcels of unsweetened chocolate in tins
6 pencils with covers.

I could hardly say that I had a ‘comfortable allowance’, it was as much as I could do to make my thirty shillings a week keep us going, so I did not feel any of this referred to me.

As soon as I got home I opened a letter from Stratford to find that a boy I had known there had been killed at Mons. I could not believe it was true. He had been at school with my brother, and he and Rex Warneford (later to win a V.C.) used to come to tea in the rectory days. People were trying to convince themselves that this was a ‘Holy War’, and that the Huns were the Blond Beast who loved evil, and the English were fighting a crusade. It did not seem to matter much what you called it, for it all amounted to the same thing in the long run.

I went to the cinema the first night house, the days shortening and winter at hand. I shrank from the walk alone across the common, and the wait at the station, but a soldier was in the waiting-room and we got talking. He was a ‘regular’ and he thought that he was very lucky to have got back. I asked him what had happened at Mons, for it was all something of a mystery still.

‘I was there,’ he said, then: ‘The ground was scarlet with blood. Like poppies. You could smell it in the air.’

I tried to conceal my own natural horror, and murmured something about his good fortune in getting away alive.

‘Yes,’ he said, ‘but that was the angels,’ and he lifted a bandaged hand which moved uneasily.

‘You’ve hurt your hand?’

'That was shrapnel.'

'What is that?' I asked him.

'Bits of shell. The doctors got it out, and I'm all right, it's just a bit difficult at times, that's all.'

'What was it about the angels?' I asked.

'You won't believe me if I tell you.'

'I don't see why not.'

He said: 'I couldn't believe it was happening. We were fighting on, just waiting to be killed, because that was what it meant. There was a gap in the lines, then, when I looked again, there was no gap, for the angels were there. They fought with swords, I saw the light on them. Lovely they looked. Like a phantom host! We cheered them. Then the order to retreat came, and I thought the Huns would shoot us down as we went. They didn't. The angels stopped that.'

The train came in.

In 1919 when I was working as a V.A.D. at the Convalescent Home at Turret Lodge, Frinton, under Miss Phyllis Holman, a hoary old war-scarred major spoke of them, too. I had been talking to him when I took him his tea, and I said, 'The angels of Mons were gun-smoke, or mirage, weren't they?'

He turned on me, and he said: 'Nobody shall ever say that in my presence, my girl. The angels of Mons saved my life. I saw them.'

Perhaps it is easy when listening to their story to mistrust the truth. I believe the angels *were*.

A new operator had now taken Lovering's place at the cinema, and the messages which I had to scratch on the slides became wearyingly disastrous. Already I was sick of the beastly war. The continual changing of our frontline was perplexing, nobody knew what was happening, and Mother with her *Daily Mail* war map (price sixpence) was in a continual dither not knowing where to put the next flag. There was a rumour that von Kluck's First Army was almost outside the fortifications of Paris.

'We simply can't put that on the slide,' I told Mr. Clements, 'it'll upset everybody and do no good.'

'They'll have to know some time or another.'

'But – but what shall we do if France falls?'

'It *will* fall,' he said, 'the sooner they realize it the better it will be.'

We had a comedy film coming on immediately after the war slides, and I knew this would ruin the big picture for everybody, but I put it on, to be received in icy silence. 'We've got the Navy,' I kept telling myself, 'something unexpected will happen. And anyway, soon it'll be Christmas, and then it'll all be over.'

We had plunged into October but we seemed to be no nearer the end. If only we could have got a clear picture! But that was impossible.

Paper money was issued and we felt this to be a positive insult to the Crown. Although other nations had used rather dirty little bits of paper money for years, we had thought of it as being common (anyway they couldn't afford anything better!) and most un-English. Yet here it was in our midst! It fluttered uneasily out of the purse given half a chance, and those of us who were not careful lost it. The penny bloater now changed to twopence-half-penny, and bang went a good breakfast! Butter and margarine kept rising. Already the war had come as an excuse for shoddiness. My old winter coat would have to do, for whatever happened one must not spend any unnecessary money, and the papers kept preaching economy. More frugal food, and heaven knows ours had always been sparse enough. We had to go nearer the bone.

Three bombs had been dropped on us. The Zepps came over. The old trouble of the spies had blazed up, and there had been mob scenes here and there. On the 19th, this was mentioned in the *Daily Mail*:

THE ENEMY IN OUR MIDST

> We have no sympathy whatever with the violent attacks that have been made in Deptford and elsewhere upon shops whose proprietors bear German names. Mob law is detestable, if only because it is utterly incapable of discrimination, and hits out blindly and without even the practice of an enquiry.

England seemed to have changed. Robert Blatchford was writing for the *Weekly Dispatch* and every Sunday we bought it only to read what he had to say, though he told us little. 'No price is too great for Calais' was the cry.

It seemed strange in the midst of a convulsive country that Pauline Chase, the first Peter Pan, the boy who never grew up (we had rather felt the actress was the same), got married on October the 24th. I read about it with affection. Yet as I glanced across the news-sheet I became horrified to read that Conan Doyle (another great pet of mine) was accused of pro-enemy leanings, for he had contributed to funds for the Committee for Assistance to Germans, Austrians and Hungarians in distress.

We seemed to be pretty pitiless in a blind urge for justice, and where were we getting? Nowhere. Prince Louis of Battenberg resigned from his position as First Sea Lord on October the thirtieth, and the headline was *'Birth an ineradicable difficulty'*. Churchill praised him, and he would receive honours from the King, but under it all lay the fact that at this particular time hatred seemed so dominant. One must not be a German at any cost.

I was feeling dreadfully ill. The breaking off of my

engagement had not helped, and I dared not let Mother know how easily I became tired, and how every little duty was a labour.

The man whom I should marry in 1916, Arthur Denham-Cookes, was having great trials with his own mother. She was a neurotic lady who enjoyed being an invalid, and kept imploring him to do nothing dangerous or she would have another attack.

The big house, No. 6 Prince's Gate, was busy with entertainment for the troops. Tea-parties were given. Amateur society belles sang or played the piano, or tried to be amusing. Arthur and the General attended some of these parties, he horrified, the General stony, and in the end they always tore themselves away from the entertainment in the drawing-room with the tommies sitting on spidery-legged gilt chairs, and went to the dining-room (where forty could dine with ease), armed with the key to the tantalus.

The man who was going to be my second husband was having an exacting time at sea. In the September he had written:

> *September the 2nd. At Sea*
> The ship mooning about all day doing nothing in particular. General Quarters in the afternoon. Had quite an exciting middle watch this morning. All kinds of ships were stopped and searched; we had to chase one ourselves.
>
> *September the 10th. At Sea*
> We had quite an exciting day. We got down to within about forty miles of Heligoland at 6.30 a.m., still going S.E. Went to action stations at 7 as a squadron of German cruisers were supposed to be knocking around. However, we missed them in a very thick fog which came down. At noon we were attacked by submarines, one of

which we sank and got no damage ourselves. We then turned back to Scapa. Had the second part of the first watch last night.

Sea, Friday the 11th
On our way back to Scapa all day. There was a bit of entertainment in the afternoon when we found we had steamed right into the middle of a field of floating mines. We all had to stop and send away boats to pick them up. Rotten day. Had the second part of the middle [watch] last night.

October was a dreary month which trailed on and on. We didn't seem to be getting anywhere on the front, and all manner of alarming stories kept going the rounds, but the spy bother in England seemed to be the great worry. Suddenly the papers spoke of Carl Hans Lody, convicted of espionage by court martial, and shot on Guy Fawkes Day in the Tower.

'Serve him right!' said everybody.

I don't know why, but this was something of a shock to me. I hated the thought of anybody being shot. It was bad enough in battle, where they took their chance side by side, but it seemed all wrong in cold blood.

'Darling, you really are quite dotty,' said Mother.

Two nights later, just as the evening programme was ending, I felt odd, and the tin clock began to smudge on the top of the piano. I managed to get through the King, and knew no more.

I had fainted across the keyboard.

Everything happened surprisingly quickly. It seemed to be within only a few days. Mother made a great decision. She saw that I was nearing a breakdown, doing far too much, and she called in Dr. Kinloch who was a darling. He thought that St. Albans was too closely associated with my broken engagement, and suggested that we should get away, right away if possible. Mother had some hazy idea of going to the east coast. The war scare had meant that one could get one's pick of houses there, dozens were going for a song, and rents down to nothing, which was just what we could afford.

Also when we thought about it, we realized that next year perhaps we could turn the house into a money-making concern. We could take P.G.s, because by 1915 the war was bound to be over. Whilst I finished up at the cinema, with some regrets I must say, Mother made one or two expeditions to the coast and finally took a Queen Anne house in Saville Street at Walton-on-the-Naze. It had seven bedrooms, a rather dubious bathroom, a big sitting-room, and small back dining-room, at the rent of twenty- five pounds a year! Rates seven!

I handed in my resignation. I wept because I had enjoyed working at the White Palace, even those pathetic times when for an extra exciting picture we engaged a 'cellist and a violinist and I had to write out band parts. The whole of the week-end would be occupied with doing this, and half Monday morning in rehearsal. Then for a week we three played. The gentlemen who lent stringed assistance would wander off during the supporting programme into the local, and come back smelling of beer, and in such an amiably benign mood, or so chatty, that I was horrified. I was too young to cope with this, and did not know what to do. It is difficult to shut up the obstreperous person when the music has to go on. I would bang away at the 'Caliph of Baghdad', and mutter 'Stop it. Stop it,' as fiercely as I could, but it was not much good.

I played 'the King' for the last time. I had already said goodbye to Mr. Clements, wondering whether after all I had done there would be something extra in my pay envelope. But I had already hoped that for a couple of

Christmases, and threepence had been the extra, which was hardly inspiring. I locked up and came away for the last time, to go up to the station with the evening paper. Lord Roberts had died suddenly in France. I don't know why, but that worried me. As a very small child I had remembered the tremendous inspiration of 'Bobs', somebody had given me a khaki sugar soldier (said to be Bobs) and I was torn between the greedy desire to eat it, and the patriotic burning to keep it for ever. Lord Roberts would be buried in the crypt of St. Paul's, where Nelson lay, and his death did bring a personal feeling of loss to us all, I am sure.

The recruiting offices took a cue from it. Out came the new poster to force white-livered young gentlemen to enlist.

He did his Duty
Will you do Yours?

Only ten days later we went down to Walton-by-the-Naze. The furniture would come along in a horse van, it would take a week and cost eleven pounds, which we thought wildly expensive, but it had to be met. We got to Walton about seven in the evening, and seemed to be entering a new world. There was the eternal music of the sea, at that time I thought it was always like that, not realizing what it could do. Mother when she married my father had gone with him to his curacy at Harwich and knew better.

'You can never trust the sea,' she said.

Everyone was arranging and rearranging blackout curtains because the streets were shadowed by 'Specials' who came round bawling, 'Light showing!' 'Put that light out!' We went into rooms next door, very comfortable and friendly they were, and next morning for the first time I saw the house where we were going to live. I loved it. It was spacious, and had great comfort, and whereas the back looked out across the backwater, then with windmills, and the old Dutch mill sparkling in the vivid autumn sun, the front looked over bare open ground to the shore. There was bleached grass, and surf and sand.

'I shall like this,' I said.

That very night the sea got up. The noise of the waves breaking on the open ground before the house was like gunfire, and even though the windows were all closed, the place got full of blown sand and smelt brackish for days. We were exhausted from moving in, until I fixed on the happy idea of putting everything about which we were not sure into one of the bedrooms, and locking the door. I had trouble with getting curtains fixed, for the windows were very tall.

The sea, who was a stranger to me, *did* alarm me. The noise it made being new to me, I could not sleep in my room at the back of the house, and thinking Mother might be awake, I sneaked out. There was a streak of light under her door, and I went in. She was sitting up in bed looking very haggard, her eyes receded into dark sockets.

'Is – is something the matter?' I asked.

When she could speak, she said: 'I didn't want to tell you till the morning, but there's a lump. It's come back.'

I gave a little gasp, then pulled myself together. 'It may be nothing. It's easy to imagine things, one never knows.'

That seemed to help her, though heaven knows why.

She said she thought that her outworn corsets had grated and could have caused it. I got into her bed, my work-basket with me. I removed the steel busks for her, replacing them with hooks and eyes. I had forgotten the noise the sea was making, I felt sick, not myself at all, but however I felt she must not know. From three that morning both of us played a game pretending that it was the storm that had disturbed us.

A rocket spat into the sky. Quickly the lifeboat went out into a raging sea which now broke high over the ground before the house, and with morning we knew that there had been a wreck at Harwich. Thirty men on leave, and one officer, had gone back to their ship, and the boat had gone down. With the jaundiced light of a sallow new day Mother said: 'You'll get a doctor, then we'll know. Anyway that will be something.'

'I'm going right now,' I promised her.

The milkman had told me where the doctor lived, and I went out. With morning the open sea was pale green, churned into ugly hills and dales, growling as it broke. The tide had gone out. A coastguard stopped me at the end of the road, where it joined the esplanade.

'I'd keep off the front, miss,' he said.

'I have to go for the doctor.'

'The beach is no place for a young lady this morning. The picket-boat from H.M.S. *Conquest* was wrecked off the Naze in the storm and the chaps are coming in. It isn't right for you, miss.'

As he said it a horse and cart clopped along past me, a Sea Scout leading it, and a coastguard with a bearded face marching beside it. A Union Jack was flung over a lump in the back of the cart, and from under it there stuck out a bluejacket's stiff leg, dripping with water. It seemed to me that the dark line of water along the road marked his brief life, and I guessed that he would have been very little older than I was.

I walked on, but a desperate urge to look back forced me and I saw the beach at low tide, with dead men lying there, crumpled men, unreal yet starkly real. It was the first time I had seen death, and the storm-seared, wreck-spattered beach was humped with men who were not men any more.

It was useless to stand retching by a tamarisk hedge, I had to find the strange doctor and beg him to be kind to

Mother. Not to let her know if it was, and already I was sure that it was. The doctor was not too kind. He said thousands of people died of cancer, and it did come back. I must pull up my socks.

In the next few days I did not have much time to worry about the war, or the young men who had been drowned, for I was so much more worried about my mother. She was to have an immediate operation in the house. The district nurse would come in for it, and Mr. Percy Coleman a surgeon from Clacton would do it. I sent for my father, for I thought he should be with us in this, and the night before the operation I went up to the station to meet him. It was another of those wild and noisy nights with a storm. In the last few days I had formed quite a different opinion of the cruelty of the sea.

The train was late and I stood in a corner of the little station on the cliff edge, with the wind shrieking and the noise of the waves like continuous thunder. With the blind faith of the young I prayed for Mother's life. If only she could live longer, just a little time more! I loved her so much and at the back of my mind was the feeling that, if I had not gone against her in becoming engaged to Montie and insisting on it, this would not have happened. I blamed myself.

My father had not wanted to come down, but we walked back to the house together. I got him some supper and then we had a talk. It couldn't be a happy one, try as we would. Next morning he and I prepared Mother's room and brought up the kitchen table which looked ominous. The district nurse arrived and took charge and he and I went downstairs.

Waiting for the operation to begin could not be a very happy time, we talked banalities, but when the surgeon came he was quick. We sat in the room listening to every sound they made above us, hating it, scared, not knowing how to help, trying to talk about the war or the weather, or something quite unimportant. When they came down to tea which I had got ready for them, the surgeon spoke to me about it.

'She ought to live two years,' he told me.

I suppose he did not know that I had expected much more. I tried not to show what I felt. 'Two years?' I repeated dimly.

'I'm sure you want the truth.' Then perhaps he noticed that I had gone pale and he said: 'You'll marry, you know. You are a very pretty girl, but you don't need me to tell you that. You'll be all right.'

'It's Mother who matters,' I murmured.

They got talking to my father, and feeling sick I went out and down to the beach. Mother would not be conscious again for an hour, they told me, and this had given me the chance to think. I sat on the dry sand, the only person who would come here on an early December afternoon, but I had wanted to be alone. Then I knew that I was not alone, for the horror had happened again. A man in a blue suit lay at the water's edge almost as if asleep. The waves came to and fro, playing with him like a cat's paw curling round the mouse she had destroyed, amusedly. Against his stillness the perpetual movement of the water was somehow horrifying.

I got up quickly, stumbling through the loose sand, and by the parapet a Sea Scout stood whittling a stick with a jack-knife. I called to him.

'There's something down there.'

He would have been about sixteen years old, I suppose; he glanced, then said: 'Oh, that's another from the Harwich wreck, I expect. You'd better go home, miss. No good hanging about here.'

I went home. I had suddenly been jolted into the ugly side of the war, something which I had never thought could happen, leastways to me.

I sat up with Mother that night, she was not properly conscious until about three, and the next night she had a relapse and I had to go out to find the district nurse for her. She rallied within the week, and from that time there we were playing a cat-and-mouse game with each other, and the shocking part was that we both knew it.

Within that same week we heard the terrible noise of gunfire, and thought there had been a battle at sea, but it was the German ships shelling the coast. It was a calamity to have arrived here only to find it far more dangerous than we had thought possible. Now my one terror was that the ships might come again and shell us before Mother was fit to get up and about again.

It was at this very time that the young snottie whom I should marry in 1925, got busy about the shelling.

> *Rosyth – Sea. December the 16th*
> Got a message from the Admiralty at 9 a.m. saying that some German battle cruisers and light cruisers had been bombarding Scarborough and had smashed the wireless station. So we got under way immediately, and were outside the Firth doing 17 knots at 10. Went to action stations as it was rather misty. Later on the Admiralty sent a message to say that the whole German High Sea Fleet was at sea, and we have been expecting an action all day but nothing has happened yet.
>
> *December the 17th. Sea*
> Had the first dog in the main top last night, and from 8 to 9.15 on the bridge. Went to action stations at daybreak and remained there until 10. At noon the chase was definitely given up and we had one or two P.Z.s and then turned back to Rosyth. Altogether a very tame and disappointing ending to a situation that promised so much.

He was bursting with patriotic fervour for the fight, which was already sickening me.

The other gentleman who was to come first into my life was having little troubles from his last sojourn at Trinity Hall, Cambridge. A waitress in a restaurant in K.P. was threatening him with a breach of promise, which – if ever she found out – would kill his mamma, he was sure. Another young lady had made him a handsome present of a sword, and as he was not mad about the one he had got he was waiting for it. When it arrived it was a cavalry sword and he was in an infantry regiment. Going back surreptitiously to the sword-maker where he understood it had been bought, and who was a first-class man, he discovered it had not been bought there at all, but happened to be one her brother did not want and she had passed it on.

His Christmas looked like being complicated, for not only this, but as all his family went in for composition (his aunt Lady Arthur Hill had written 'In the Gloaming, Oh my darling', his uncle Lord Lurgan composed beautifully, and his son Brownie (the present Lord Lurgan) was musically most gifted), so Arthur Denham-Cookes had written a waltz. The war had held up publication, and it appeared in the December, he having completely forgotten about it, only to recall in horror that being a waltz and the Austrians and Germans being closely associated with such, he had published it under a German pseudonym, Rudolph Ausberg.

He and the butler burnt the lot before anybody saw.

'This isn't my war,' said Arthur.

At Walton, Mother was slowly getting about again. The anxiety was not lifting. She was to go to London for radium treatment in January, and the surgeon held out great hope. I wonder if we really had any hope left, I doubt it, but we had to go on.

Joscelyn was lucky in that he got Christmas leave. The first stage of passionate enthusiasm was dead, and we knew that the Herts. R.F.A. were posted for overseas duties in February, also it would be to France. France was icebound at the moment, but with the spring the war would flare up anew, anything might happen. Christmas, the time when it was all going to be over, had been a snare and a delusion.

I went to meet my brother at the station, and it happened to be one of those Christmases when we were particularly short of money. It would be his final leave, and we knew he felt dreadful about it, as indeed did we both.

On Christmas Day we ate cold ham round the fire, and played Double Dummy patience all the afternoon. Mother in a fit of wild generosity, which I am sure she could not afford, was giving half-a-crown to the first person who won it four times running.

It was bad weather, and the leave petered out, accomplishing little, and not making any of us very happy really, seeing that it might be the last time we should ever see Joscelyn. Mercifully Mother was too weak to go to the station with him, so I went alone.

The novelty was tarnishing. Once the fact of having a brother in Fred Karno's Army and going abroad to fight was a triumph, now it was not quite so great. We felt miserable.

It was one of those grey days which in winter frequent the east coast and are inescapable. We discussed the weather, the Radium Institute where Mother was going next week, anything rather than the fact that he was going away. I remember that he looked considerably older, and wore corporal's stripes. When the train came I pressed the only half-crown that I possessed into his hand and waved him away, then turned to walk home, the mist gathering on the sea.

There was some comfort in the realization that we were fighting this war so that no other people would ever have to fight again, but when you are actually doing it even the strong sense of a duty done is insufficient to give you heart. Mother sat by the fire, she looked very drawn and grey. We sat on playing patience until supper-time – supper was broken biscuits.

We went up at once to the Radium Institute in Riding House Street, to stay in a ladies' hostel in Gower Street where they took us in for nineteen-and-nine a week (cubicled room for three, and the third was a French lady who made an awful noise when she cleaned her teeth). Mother spent so many hours a day at the Radium Institute under Mr. Pinch, and it was an exhausting treatment, she feeling ill all the time. Because she was a clergyman's wife they treated her more than kindly and we paid so little that it was hardly a fee at all. But the bother lay in the taxis to and fro (she could not travel by bus) and the railway fare, which, even if these cost the least possible, were still too much for us on an income of £120 a year.

The new year was greeted excitedly, and the leader writer in the *Daily Mail* on January the first wrote:

> A year opens today that will decide, or go a long way to deciding, the destination of Europe for many decades to come.

The sales had started, and I read the advertisements with an avid eye, for dress appealed to me. Whiteley's had Russian real pony-skin coats reduced from nine and a half guineas to six. The tea frock had come into vogue, very chiffony and attractive and awfully mature-looking, which made me eager for it.

The new struggle for Ypres had begun. The papers seemed gloomy, and even the fascinations of the advertisements for the winter sales could not entirely dim the fact that the new year was not starting well.

At Walton when the world was quite still in the very early mornings we could, if the wind was the right way, frequently hear the heavy booming of the guns in France. The earth vibrated with it, and we knew that an offensive had started. Then one day it seemed to be considerably nearer, quite alarmingly so.

'Possibly a mine at sea?' I suggested.

'Oh no,' said Mother, 'that's quite another sound, it isn't guns across the Channel, I think that it is something here.'

Next day we knew what had happened, for the paper told us that the Zepps had been over, bombing Great Yarmouth, Cromer, and King's Lynn. All along we had felt sure that an attack from the air must come, and in one way there was the sense of satisfaction, 'Thank goodness, now it is here at last!' Mother went down and got the paper early from the mat, and when I went in to see her she was sitting up in bed reading it.

'This is only the start,' she insisted. 'I always knew that flying was a ghastly mistake, and we'll all be in the front line now.'

The Zeppelin raid on Norfolk was treated almost as if it had been an invasion. Public feeling became agitated, and security regulations were tightened, making the restrictions increasingly severe, and we were having further trouble with skimpy curtains which would not fit in spite of the ubiquitous safety-pin. At night the 'Specials' were busy as bees in a hive, and where once a little chink had not mattered, now the merest suggestion of it brought them hammering on the door, and making rude remarks.

If raiders came the Scouts would give the warning on their bicycles, and their bugles later would give the All Clear. This was undoubtedly the Scouts' war. Not only had they been called up for war duties on August the fourth last year, but they were still at them. Mother was concerned that the Sea Scouts had to rescue bodies from the beach or sea and take them to the mortuary behind the cemetery; she felt that this was shocking for boys who were so young, but then the whole of the war was shocking, and most of all for youth.

The onus of the casualty lists seemed to be borne mainly by the second lieutenants who were being mown down all the time. More and more women in mourning filled the streets, for it was the era of mourning which had to be worn for the regulation time at all costs. Deep mourning for a year for close relatives, half-mourning (grey, white or purple) for the subsequent year, and widows' weeds were necessary for a year and a day. Heaven alone knows why!

The thought of Zeppelin raids made everyone think what to do for the best when it came to shelter. The main wall of the house was one suggestion. The cellar was certainly an idea, and for rich families excellent, for then Dad could get a drink when he most needed it!

The spring was coming. It might be that the glory of fighting the war to end all wars was getting a bit tarnished, and we had secret apprehensions of what this spring might bring; at the same time, perhaps we had got through the worst.

What next?

CHAPTER 6

Spring always comes late on the east coast and this one followed the pattern of its predecessors. The arrangement was that every six weeks Mother went to the hostel in Gower Street and had treatment at the Radium Institute. Anyway something was being done for her and that gave us confidence, though probably deep down within both of us the anxiety continued. How could it be otherwise?

Three times a week I played the piano at the soldiers' recreation rooms. They were dreary in some ways, for being schoolrooms by day the children's work was lying about, and the piano was always tinny. 'Little Grey Home in the West' was in great demand, 'There's a long, long trail a'winding', and 'Tipperary'. The cinema had taught me how to build up an entertaining *pot-pourri*, though often the men turned from the gay songs, and sought something utterly miserable, like 'Here a sheer hulk lies poor Tom Bowling' (since my experience on Walton beach that first day I felt strongly about that one), 'Home, Sweet Home', and 'Poor old Joe'. My work there was what was known as 'doing my bit'. The men were amazingly happy, laughing at the discomforts of billets, and always believing that the war must end fairly soon. They never seemed to be aware of the wretched fact that with the better weather, men overseas were dying right and left; that deserters were made to dig their own graves, then shot, so we were told. Life was sheer hell out there.

The men told me the difference between an officer's uniform and a private's, something I found hard to get into my head. My first instructions were that an officer always wore a Sam Browne, which led me into a regrettable error of judgement one day with a sergeant-major! The regiment stationed with us was the Essex Cyclists, an innovation for that particular war.

We waited for the spring and the big advance, with everything growing more difficult; threepenny-halfpenny tins of tinned milk were now sevenpence-halfpenny, even broken biscuits had gone up, and of course if the war did not end soon all would go up still more.

On April the twenty-second I rose early and slipped down to get the paper. The headlines were shocking. The Germans had made their first gas attack before Ypres and the thought of it sent me completely cold. Joscelyn was somewhere in the neighbourhood. I did not know what to do to keep this from Mother, she would be bound to hear of it sooner or later, but for the moment I parried that one.

I went to her and told her that Mark James (the newspaper shop) had forgotten to send the paper along this morning.

'Isn't that annoying?' said she. 'Never mind, I'll go out and get it myself when I get up.'

I said I'd go, because I could then say that they had sold out. She was annoyed about it. I read what the paper said about the first gas attack. It had come when the battle front was apparently completely peaceful, and the first sign had been a light mist along the front of the German trenches, which drove across No-Man's-Land into the Allied lines. Two French divisions had been wiped out, and the Canucks had come up to take over from them. They had no respirators or masks, and could only tie their handkerchiefs over their mouths. Later we were to know that our secret agents had reported that this gas attack was coming, and news had been sent that the gas was already stored in iron cylinders in the shell-proof shelters at the back of the German trenches, yet nobody had done anything about it.

I thought that I had been clever in keeping Mother in the dark, but when we went on to the front with our needlework an old man we knew came along.

'It's awful about this gas,' he said. 'Them Germans, and this gas attack on our poor boys!'

Mother looked at him, her face ashy, but she spoke almost without fear. 'They haven't used gas, surely?'

'Oh, they have, ma'am, and they'll do it again, you may be sure.' He stumped off along the front. She said nothing for a moment, then she turned to me.

'It was nice of you keeping the paper from me, dear, but you can't keep the truth from people. The time comes when you have to admit it. What a shocking thing it all is!' Neither of us had mentioned Joscelyn, I suppose we dare not, and now I was terrified lest a War Office telegram would come. In a few days we heard, and we gathered that in his particular neighbourhood nothing had happened; he and Harold had stitched away in the saddlers' shop noticing nothing amiss.

By the same post I received a letter from Montie who was being sent overseas. He was now a second lieutenant, the rank which topped the casualty lists, and that thought in itself was disturbing. He asked if he could come down for a night to say goodbye, and I asked Mother, sure that she would say no, but she said yes.

I went up to the station to meet him and we walked down the sea-front to the house together. I had to admit that I felt strange and awkward, vaguely embarrassed, and he seemed to be considerably changed. He told me that he had joined what was known as the Suicide Club in the Army, a band of young men who volunteered for dangerous duties in the course of which they died like flies. He expected to be sent out to India but knew nothing for certain.

We supped at home, Mother going to bed early, for she felt weak, at the end of a course of radium, and the reaction was severe. Montie was sympathetic. He thought it dreadful for me to be living this way and had come down with a plan. Would I marry him before he sailed and so get the marriage allowance? I sat in the sitting-room which gave the impression of affluence (an impression which had at all costs to be maintained), and I tried to think that this was one of the big moments in my life, all the time knowing that it was not. The whole of my future could change now, and suddenly I knew that I couldn't do it. In a sense I had grown away from him; this had come too late.

'I'm so sorry,' I said, 'but I can't do it.'

He mentioned it again next day when we walked up to the station together, and I went into it more fully. I blamed myself for that unhappiness which perhaps had precipitated the return of Mother's illness, so I had dedicated myself to her; whatever she wanted I would do, but somehow I did not think that she would want me to marry him.

We said goodbye calmly. I walked back and Mother was waiting at the gate. Her eyes interrogated me, she had a way of always knowing things about me, so I told her.

'He asked me to marry him and I said no,' I said. That was all.

We were staying in Gower Street, and the prices had gone up again, which was a blow. Twenty-three-and-six for bed and breakfast and a high-tea-supper seemed dear, we thought, for in 1914 it had cost nineteen-and-six, and they had given us bacon *and* egg for breakfast; now it was only 'egg'. We were staying there when the whole of London was shaken by the newsboys rushing through the streets with a special edition, for the Cunard liner S.S. *Lusitania* had been sunk off the coast of Ireland.

'But it *can't* be true,' I gasped, standing on the iron balcony which curled before the 'drawing-room' first-floor windows.

The *Lusitania* was a mighty name. We had not thought of her in the same way as we had thought of the unsinkable *Titanic*, but she certainly had been the next best thing. Her mission overseas had been harmless, and it seemed impossible that she could have been sunk, but she had been. It had been two o'clock in the afternoon when she had been torpedoed off Kinsale, had quivered, then turned on her side. She had gone down almost at once, and only a few boats had got away. The sordid pictures showed line after line of little children lying on the floor of the mortuary; I have never forgotten it.

At that time young Gower Robinson, now getting a lot of war experience, wrote in his diary:

> *May 7th*, 1915. *At Sea*
> Been going north all day, and are now about latitude 63°, with the result that although it is just on midnight it is almost broad daylight. Sub-calibre firing in the forenoon, anti-torpedo-boat firing in the afternoon. Very cold and windy. The *Lusitania* has been sunk by the Germans, and 1,400 lives lost. How awful!

He had however recovered somewhat from the shock a few days later.

> *May 11th*, 1915. *Rosyth*
> Frightfully busy all day, so busy that I had to go without my breakfast; a proper red letter day! Very cold and wet. The *Maori* has struck a mine and has been destroyed. The Admiral has called for 'reliable and adventurous midshipmen of a mechanical turn of mind'. I wonder what for!

It seemed to me that the catastrophe of the *Lusitania* was the most horrifying thing that had yet happened, including the gas attack at Ypres. After all, at Ypres they were then attacking armed men and this murder of civilians stung us out of that period of lethargy which winter had set upon us. The news went round that this was the work of spies; the sailing date had been disclosed, and up blazed the old fanatical hatred and the mob was out for blood.

That night the crowds raided the shops which had German name-boards over them. Appenrodt's was smashed up and hundreds of sausages were bouncing about the street. Broken windows were everywhere and people injured. Next day the German sausage was renamed breakfast sausage, which it has been called ever since, and Frankfurters disappeared.

In the hostel people were vehement. They thought all Germans should be pushed out of this country, good and bad alike. A woman who went out leading a little dachshund, had it stoned to death on the pavement, for there was no stemming this ugly tide of racial hatred to which the sinking of the *Lusitania* had given rise. It eclipsed those news items which had interested us through the laggard spring: the Brides-in-the-Bath case, and George Joseph Smith remanded for trial at the Old Bailey; the amputation of Sarah Bernhardt's leg; that worry and argument about choosing a badge for the Welsh Guards, should it be a leek, a daffodil, or a dragon? Now, it seemed, we wanted blood.

Today of course it does not seem extraordinary that women and children should perish in world warfare, but then it was an affront to all the laws of civilization, and even the mildest people were up in arms about it.

As we travelled back to Walton, Mother tried to comfort my apprehensions for the future. She foresaw the war coming closer, but said that at all costs we must not become scared. She knew also that she was dying and realized I should be left entirely alone, and helpless. It was no advantage that I have always been appallingly young for my years. Perhaps she wanted my happiness more than anybody else has ever done, and she had not the power to give it to me. Through it all she never referred to her own malady, nor did she use it as an excuse. Once when she found me in my room crying about it, she came and took my hand almost commandingly.

'You must never cry about this,' she said, 'it's so silly. Lots of people we know will die before I do, it is only because you *know* that I must die that it upsets you. All of us go some day, but we don't cry about it.'

One night I was disturbed by a jangling sound like chains, and it was quite a guttural noise. I went to Mother who was awake and we thought it wiser to go downstairs. People were running about the street, the 'Specials' were busy, and whistles were being blown everywhere. We daren't turn on the gas, for I regret to say we had never managed to get those wretched curtains to fit. Out of the distance came the splutter of gunfire.

'Now what was that?' I asked.

'A bomb, I suppose,' and as the clanking guttural

sound came nearer, 'that's a Zepp speaking German.'

She became fascinated by it, and decided that the thing to do was to ensure a satisfactory front seat and sit on the doorstep, for she did not intend to miss any of it. Out we went, I dithering, but Mother treating it as if it were a Command Performance for which someone had sent her a free ticket.

It was a warm night with people everywhere. I heard a shriek of wrath from an outraged spectator because one miserable man lit a cigarette. 'We might all have died for that there,' he screamed.

Three cigar-shaped airships were in the sky over Harwich, and the Dovercourt-Harwich peninsula on the far side of the backwater seemed to have caught fire. It blazed defiantly and the ominous copper reflection was eerie. Every now and then one of the big cigars swerved round and came lumbering our way, croaking as it came, then went back to the target.

'It's absorbing,' said Mother. 'I wouldn't have missed it for the world.'

It lasted about an hour, then through the night came a small British plane, like an irritatingly buzzing little bee. If the thing was a midget, and it looked it, it had the courage of a giant. It began shooting, making pop-gun noises against the heavy thud of bombs. Some of us prayed for the gallant young man who was risking his life in that rickety little plane and shooting only with a pistol. The miracle happened.

One of the Zepps hovering round made a new sound. Her engine missed fire, she lurched cock-eyed to one side, recovered, lurched again, then edged off making ghastly noises. We screamed: 'Bravo, bravo! Go on, go on, go on!' and that young man *did* go on; how he ever kept up I cannot think. It was the first battle of my life, I wish to heaven it had been my last.

Ten minutes later when the peninsula was a dart of

scarlet flame and copper glow, we heard the bugles of the Sea Scouts telling us we were safe again.

We went up to bed, and I had gone limp. I supposed this was something one associated with the white feathers old ladies and pert debs gave to unhappy young men who had not joined up. I cried a little when I was alone. Only a year ago I could not have believed that such a thing was possible; in August of last year I had been proud to be in this war, now there was the uncertainty all the time, the doubts, and the apprehensions.

I prayed that the brave young man in the silly little aeroplane had not been hurt. I thought of the whining, hiccuping, wounded Zepp who had turned to the sea and who I was quite sure could never get back to Germany intact, and, anyway, the last I had seen of her was with the young man shooting madly at her. The young men in the Zepp had wives and mothers too, and although I knew that it was a shameful thing to be sorry for the Germans, I wondered what had happened to them. Had they reached the *Vaterland* safely?

Of course we wanted all Germans to be killed, but lying in bed there with the sound of the sea coming into the room, the recurring thought came to me: *What had happened to those young men?*

If food prices went up with the war, the price of clothes did not rise in the same way. Longcloth nightdresses with a lot of remarkable *broderie anglaise* on them were still only four-and-six, glacé ward shoes only two-and-six, and I could buy a pleasant hat for a shilling, a vest for one-and-six, and enough white voile to make myself a blouse for one-and-nine. (Voile was the mode.)

After that Zepp raid, whenever Mother had to return to London for further treatment she took me with her, not liking to leave me behind. I loved staying in London, and when she was in the Radium Institute I walked miles because I could not afford the bus fares, but I found it the greatest fun. Privately I had been afraid of being left alone in Hertford House, never liking the dark and being even more alarmed at the thought of ghosts than I was over Germans. Some idiot had told me that the house was well known to be haunted. It was untrue, for we never saw anything whilst we were there, and the only haunting was by the ants which we could not keep out of the larder and which at times drove us crazy.

I was enjoying the Brides-in-the-Bath case which was now being heard at the Old Bailey. Everybody argued for hours about it, though at heart we all thought George Joseph Smith was a horrid man who had done it entirely for money, which is perhaps the lowest form of murder of them all.

I was becoming more nervous about my mother's condition. The nurses and doctors at Riding House Street were friendly, and at first I had been misled by the hopefulness of their demeanour and had not realized it was their cunning armour against too close enquiry. It was evasion. Mother, I gathered, had not recognized this, or if she had done was herself also pretending. But this gallant game of pretence probably on both sides was hard to play, particularly as I think each of us knew we must lose in the long run.

One afternoon when she was away I sat in the drawing-room of the ladies' hostel and I heard the sound of obstreperous singing coming along Gower Street. For one moment I thought perhaps the war was over, and went on to the balcony. The noise came from a crowd dancing up the street, and all the Italians from the Italian quarter were romping towards me, arms linked like a lot of children playing Nuts in May. They waved small flags, they sang, and I rushed out to join them. Suddenly in that moment I realized that for months now I had been starved for fun, for youth, and for joy, and here it was in the street itself.

'What's it all about?' I asked.

An Italian pushing a hurdy-gurdy in the gutter took off a huge fusty hat and bowed. '*Signorita*, we are the companion. We fight together,' and he beat his hairy chest – his shirt was open – like a gorilla.

This is victory at last, thought I, and in an instant had attached myself to the tail end of the dancers and off we went. They sang, and I sang too. As we pranced up the street amorous young men indicated my fair hair, saying: *'Bella! Bella!'* I felt *bella*! I stole an Italian flag from somewhere, and I did a *pas seul* round a lamp-post with it. *'Brava. Brava,'* clapped my gay associates. War was fun! Victory was sweet! What a thrill that was!

We danced into the Euston Road, hopped round Maple's and gavotted back into Torrington Place, all of us together, and what did anything matter save the sheer joy of the moment? When I returned to the hostel my hair was half down, a dreadful ignominy for such an era, my blouse was torn, for in a quicksilver here-we-go-round-and-round someone had snatched at it hoping it would act as a brake. I had confetti down my neck, and I did not think that my mother would consider any of this was quite the thing to do.

The last time we had stayed here I and some medical student friends from University College Hospital had heard an all-masculine crowd approaching, and had rushed out in defence of Phineas, the effigy in the hospital courtyard. That *had* been a fight, and we had come down Gower Street, Phineas and all, then up Gower Street, Phineas and all, and I had been found prostrate in the gutter, having done little to defend Phineas, but nobody could say that I hadn't tried. Mother had been annoyed. The fight was far too male for me, and I admit that I was bruised for days.

But the Italians were *in* the war. If I could not find the money to get into the gallery and see *Potash and Perlmutter* at the Queen's Theatre, at least I had had some entertainment. And as I kept telling myself, surely this must mean that victory was in sight?

CHAPTER 7

At this time Arthur Denham-Cookes was involved in the move which would bring him down to Walton-on-the-Naze to meet me and to marry. So far his war had been plain sailing, save that he found the General trying at times. The regiment were stationed at Bishop's Stortford, which was close enough to London for them to come up for entertainment there almost nightly, and to enjoy themselves. There was, however, trouble ahead. The General went out to meet another general who was his senior in rank, and they got wrong. The two aides commiserated with each other; the start of the row was the rice pudding Arthur's General had wanted and didn't get, and about which he was extremely rude.

The old gentleman (he seemed very old to me when I met him) having been Indian Army, had the internal condition to which Rudyard Kipling referred so aptly as having 'liver and lights like lead', and he had to be careful about his choice of puddings. The two aides became seconds in a fight, and the cad who was the senior general behaved like a swine. As Arthur put it,

'He *would* have to kick up a dust at the War Office.'

Arthur's General became a brigadier-general and was sent home (I have always regretted that I never knew exactly what it was he said), and Arthur ceased to be an aide, and was now on the move which was to bring him to Walton-on-the-Naze where the Queen's took over from the Essex Cyclists.

The other young man who later would be preoccupying my life seemed to be closer to the real war.

> *Sea – Sheerness*
> A most exciting day following the swept channel nearly all day, with four destroyers escorting us. Endless messages coming through saying that submarines had been sighted a few miles ahead of us, and mines as well. Very nearly had a collision with a collier which crossed our bows. Got into Sheerness at 2100, and half of us went on leave.
>
> *Sheerness – Chatham – Home*
> Came up this morning and exactly 12 hours later I was throwing mud up at mother's window trying to wake her after a very large supper at Victoria station.

We returned to Walton, and it seemed that the explosions out at sea grew worse.

Soldiers were working day and night building heavy sandbag reinforcements all along the front, and some of the cliff between us and Frinton collapsed through their strenuous efforts.

It was then that I wrote youthfully and glowingly to my father, explaining how very much I was enjoying the excitement of the moment.

Hertford House,
Saville Street,
Walton-on-the-Naze
July the 4th, 1915

Dear Dad,

It is tremendously exciting at times here, and things are always happening. I hear great-Aunt Fenella slept two hours in the cellar in her nightdress, bombs all around her at Woodbridge; she must have had a scare, poor dear! Yesterday we could hear them dropping bombs to the south of us, Southend, we fancied, and last Sunday destroyers went past and took 3 German submarine into Harwich. It was such fun, you'd have loved it. By the by, I suppose we *are* going to win the war? I mean it does seem to be going on for a beastly long time, what do you really think?

I am embroidering a cushion cover for you, and the colours all wash, so you need not worry about it.

With love,

URSULA

We would sit most of the day doing crochet on the front (in the Marine Gardens), watching the soldiers working on the sandbags, and listening to the distant gunfire. 'Practice' was what Mother always said, in case I got worried, but I think half of it was most certainly *not* practice.

In the middle of the month my father wrote to me.

Whitchurch Rectory,
Stratford-on-Avon.
July the Fourteenth, 1915

Dearest Ursula,

I have got to come down to Walton to see both you and your mother about something which I think is very serious, and the sooner we all have a talk the better. You are in considerable danger. Don't mention this, or talk to any soldiers, until I have seen you. I have had a long confidential letter from the Bishop of Worcester which I cannot divulge but which deals with your behaviour at Walton, and I think that the best thing I can do is to come to see you immediately.

I ought to be with you the evening of the day on which you receive this, and the train arrives at 6.20. Please meet me so that we can chat before your mother knows. This is most important for your safety.

Your affectionate

DAD

I showed the letter immediately to my mother, and she could not imagine what it was about. She thought my father must have gone mad, and what he meant by 'our behaviour at Walton' completely mystified us both. Ours had been the most simple life; we had in fact been so impoverished that there was practically nothing that we could have done.

My routine life had been spent in nursing Mother, in getting her out on to the front about eleven on sunny mornings and sitting there talking to her, or writing stories. After lunch she always had a long rest; in the evening officers and their wives came in for coffee and drinks. Whisky was still mercifully cheap, and I bought 'The Three Gees' at the International Stores for three-and-six a bottle. If we went without lunch for a week, we could contrive an evening with drinks.

We could not think that anything could have gone wrong, yet according to my father's letter it most certainly had. But how had the Bishop of Worcester become involved?

'It's no good trying to work it out,' said my mother, 'your father must have flown off at a tangent and has got hold of the wrong idea.'

That evening I went up to the station to meet him. It was another of those lovely nacre-coloured evenings, when you could not believe that such a sinister thing as this wretched war even existed. The train was late, it was a single line from Thorpe-le-Soken and never hurried itself too much; when my father stepped off it in his grey flannel suit, I had to admit that he looked worried.

We walked out of the station down to the sea-front, and I showed him the reinforcements on which the soldiers had worked so hard, thinking this would interest him. It had quite the contrary effect, for he stared at me in complete horror and said would I please not mention anything of the sort?

'But why not?' I asked. 'They are here for everybody to see; there's nothing secret about them, and we all talk about them.'

'Not now, please. Please *not now*,' said he.

When we reached Mr. Barker's Marine Hotel, an amiable old-fashioned building with the public gardens before it, I think he had come to the conclusion that he had better get the object of his visit off his chest, so we went into the gardens and sat down there to talk.

He said: 'Ursula, you've got to know, but something dreadful has happened. A letter has been sent to the Bishop by someone from Walton who asked that their identity should not be disclosed. They wanted to know if you and your mother were wife and daughter of a clergyman called Bloom in Yeatman-Biggs' diocese. The Bishop wrote back and asked them why.'

'But why should anyone write to the Bishop about us?'

'I can't think. I begged him to reveal the name, but he

refused, I suppose he couldn't do more. The second letter he received made him send for me, and the upshot was that he felt this was something I must know about and act upon.'

'What did the letter say?' I asked, not seeing daylight, and thinking my father was only being silly.

'Apparently the Special Constables had had trouble with your house showing lights, and once this had coincided with a Zeppelin raid.'

'Everybody here has trouble with their lights at some time or other. Our curtains don't fit properly; they're better than they were, but they're not right yet. Why?'

'The letter said that you and your mother spent all the time on the front watching the soldiers, and disguising your real intentions by pretending to do needlework. You wrote down what you saw in an exercise book.'

'What do you mean by disguising our intentions? Of course I write in exercise books, they're my stories,' said I.

He turned his blue eyes round on me, and I saw that he was distraught. 'They suspect you of being German spies.'

'But – but how could we be?' For the first time in my life I found myself stammering.

'The name, I suppose. Bloom. It sounds German. Then you came down here as soon as the war started, and you seem to have been sitting on the front ever since. When the Zeppelins came over they said your mother tried to force her way past a Special Constable on to the front.'

'But of course she didn't. There was a plane pursuing the Zepps, and she ran down the road to see if she could get a better view from the opening by the Albion Hotel.'

'The Bishop and I are worried.'

At that moment I doubt if either of them was as worried as I was. I remembered with painful clarity that horrible night in London when the crowd had smashed some of the shops with German names over them, and the sausages had rolled into the gutters. I remembered the story of the poor little dachshund who had been stoned to death, and rather haltingly I said: 'It's – it's ridiculous. What about Joscelyn who is fighting with the British Army in France? What – what do we do?'

He didn't know, for he himself was bewildered by it, and only too anxious that we did not become further involved. 'We must all talk it out, and decide on what is the best action to take. It may mean that you'll have to leave the coast.'

I knew that I did not want to leave, somehow I had grown to care for the place, but I did not want my mother to be too worried. We walked home not in the merriest of moods. Supper was waiting and I felt some distaste for it which was odd for I had had no tea. My father told Mother what had happened. Having always been a fighter, more so than my father, her one idea was to get to the root of the matter. He thought we should retire into our shells, never go near the front, or have officers in to share coffee and three-and-sixpenny whisky.

'They know you speak German,' he said.

'So does every woman who has been to school in Bonn.'

'They know that as well. Someone has gone to a lot of trouble to find out everything they could.'

I was nervous, and because I thought they might like to talk about this alone I slipped out into the street on which the pleasant summer night had now descended. I had intended to go on to the beach, then realized that I dare not do this in case someone suspected that I was there to send messages to the enemy! In a single instant I myself had changed! I was afraid. I watched a searchlight playing in a long shaft of light which penetrated up into the sky and was afraid to be found looking. It would be easy to misinterpret my movements, and then I would become more suspect. The more I thought of it the clearer was the fact that it was extremely difficult to act innocently and behave normally.

They shoot people for this, I thought. The situation was exaggerating itself in my mind, not without reason, for at that time in the nation's history all England searched for spies, and with infuriated vigour.

Next morning I rose early to get my father's breakfast.

I had a chat with the milkman, an amiable fisherman who had already taught me the right way to cook a kipper, having caught me frying one, and going up in smoke over it himself. I wondered with horror if he had heard the scandal and what he privately thought I was. In one way I wished to do a bolt, in another I wanted to fight. It was hard to know what to do next.

That afternoon my father went for a walk to the Naze whilst Mother was resting. He was in search of geological specimens which he said were a species to be found only in this particular part of the cliffs. There was a look-out on the Naze (the tower is there today), manned, I believe, by the Royal Navy and out of bounds for all of us, though my father did not know it. Arming himself with that idiotic sponge-bag of his to contain specimens, a pocket magnifying-glass which was a treasure that went everywhere with him, and some sandwiches, he busily examined the cliffs. He became so rapt in this that he was oblivious when the look-out sentry challenged him. Unaccustomed to people yelling at him, I doubt whether even if he had heard he would have paid any attention, merely surmising that someone was being rude.

He was a middle-aged clergyman pottering after fossils, and the next thing was that they fired a shot which bounced on the ground just ahead of him. He found that surprising, if not irritating. An officer approached and questioned him, and what made my father so angry was that he had the impertinence to take his precious sponge-bag from him, also the magnifying-glass. It was some time before he could get them back, and I don't think that they would have parted with them then, save that they had come to the conclusion that nothing would make my father go away without them, and the thought of having him with them for the night was a bit too much!

When he returned to Hertford House he was purple with rage. We immediately realized that this unfortunate affair would only increase the suspicions about the Bloom family which were already boiling up. There had recently been some nasty stories in the papers about spies who had disguised themselves as clergymen (even as nuns), and we could imagine these being quoted round the hearthsides of Walton.

My father was now angry and wanted to shake the dust of the place off his feet. Most unfortunately, although we had talked of nothing else save a plan of campaign since his arrival, he left without any definite action being devised.

Mother was the one who finally determined on a plan. She was always by far the stronger fighter. She would carry on as she had begun, and so make people realize how innocent was our behaviour. But she was anxious to discover who had written the letter to the Bishop. She came to the conclusion that it could only be one of the Smiths, he was the local incumbent. The Bishop would have ignored an enquiry from a layman, and no layman would have thought of writing to him.

On our arrival at Walton Mr. and Mrs. Smith had called on us, and the call had been returned within the proper ten days and at the polite hour, which was still vital in social life. The correct cards had been left, and we had taken tea in the dark vicarage. Later they had come to tea with us and that was where the friendship had ended, for no further invitation had come and it was their turn. The 'turn' was important in the social activities of that day, and to step out of turn was to commit a gaffe.

Mother wrote frankly to Mr. Smith, saying that she had been in touch with the Bishop of Worcester with regard to the fact that a writer who wished to remain anonymous had suggested that she and her daughter were German spies. She explained her education in Bonn, that her son was serving with the B.E.F. in France, and that the Blooms were not, and never had been, anything to do with Germany, but had come from Denmark. She suggested that the best way to clear up this matter was to meet in a friendly manner, and she asked him to tea. She said that she would not be discourteous, and her only wish was to end a difficult situation.

The reply was most unpleasant.

Mr. Smith refused to deny or accept the accusation. He would not meet her, and only wished the correspondence to cease, most certainly he would not reply to any further letter from her. It was clear that he did not believe a word of what she had said about her innocence.

It sounds little today, but in that hour we were two women facing a threat which could easily be disastrous. The spy stigma was a virulent disease; it could end in arrest as a lot of other unfortunate people had already discovered.

We felt like naughty children who had been accused of a sin they had not committed, and we had no idea how to clear ourselves, or how to live through the next few weeks when it must be so very much to the fore in our minds. Fate came to the rescue in a dreadful way.

Mother went upstairs that evening to change her blouse (our loyal adherence to the old days at the rectory) and she came down looking different. Her face was ashy, her eyes had gone dark; she looked helplessly at me.

'Is something the matter?' I asked.

She sat down, for a moment not speaking, and her hands were twisted together in her lap. Then when she did speak it sounded like some rusty old door wheezed open by force. 'It's come back,' she said.

'Not another lump?'

She nodded. Whatever else went on in our lives, this malignant enemy stood his ground; it was another desperate situation about which we could do nothing.

'It can't have been there long or the radium people would have noticed it,' I said, clutching at faint hopes before they rushed past me. 'It could be a gland swollen up, or something?'

Mother shook her head. 'I suppose they'll operate again. Like this, I shall gradually be hacked to pieces.'

I said: 'Let's go round and see the doctor now? It's no good waiting for bedtime, then lying awake and thinking about it all night. Let's go round, shall we?'

She wasn't listening. I repeated it. She stayed silent for a time, then she said, 'All right.'

It was low tide and people were paddling on the beach, the children making a lot of noise. The hazy horizon told us good weather was coming, and here or there the grey smudge of a ship showed. We went to the doctor, and he saw us at once. He said it was a small thing and could be removed with a 'local', there was really nothing to worry about, for the next radium treatment would put it right. But we had seen the writing on the wall, and once one reads that, hope waves goodbye. This was the routine performance of this particular malady.

The doctor telephoned the surgeon at Clacton whilst

we were there, and he arranged to do it in Mother's bedroom as before, and it could be early next week. I doubt if either of us listened to the conversation, for we were thinking of things ahead; we had for the moment forgotten the war horrors, and the tragedy of being dubbed as spies; we thanked him and walked back. People were turning home, for we had been longer than we had thought.

'It'll be all right,' I told her, I hoped comfortingly.

In a meaningless voice she said: 'Yes, of course. It'll be all right.'

My father did not come down for this operation, really there was no need. I think privately he had been far more disturbed by the affair on the Naze than he had admitted, and he must have known he should have visited the vicar for us and have challenged him on our behalf. Mr. Smith might have told a brother in the cloth, and my father's defence would have been far more effective than anything Mother or I could hope to put up.

The only bright spot of that particular week was a letter from Joscelyn, telling us that he was in the south of France and would shortly be sailing for a secret destination. He wrote:

> I'm glad to be getting out of this and going where I know I shall like it better. I read much about it as a boy at Whitchurch, it should be interesting.

As a child Joscelyn had been amazingly interested in the Book of the Dead, and we knew at once that he would now be going to Egypt, where he would be reasonably safe.

The war was getting nowhere, and there were all sorts of troubles at home with shirkers, and with dock struggles and such. The amiable people of the world in which I lived seemed to have changed and to be showing new faces, which in itself was alarming and bewildering.

On the day of the operation, the district nurse came in, and the two doctors, and I sat alone waiting for their return with tea ready in the rather charming sitting-room of Hertford House. I felt dismally alone. I remember I picked up a paper and in it was an article by Marie Corelli, friend of my extreme youth, and she startled me by the fact that she showed fresh reasons for the present world conditions.

> The public emotionalism of the hour is apt to become rather more hysterical than reasonable, and before we begin to groan and scream in the Press about the 'unpatriotic' it might be wiser for us to consider the position dispassionately, not only from the worker's point of view, but also from that of the shirkers. The long and splendid peace enjoyed in these fortunate isles of Britain, a peace too little appreciated or gratefully recognized has created round us an atmosphere of comfort and security which has in its turn engendered personal selfishness. Like fine fruit kept too long in wadding, and beginning to deteriorate into rotten pulp, so we have hardly shown ourselves aware of anything going on outside our protective set. We have deliberately encouraged the workers not to work, just as we have deliberately encouraged our shirkers to shirk …

I, who had been brought up in an era when class was class, and had known Marie Corelli as a gifted lady who herself was not above the challenge of selfishness, was amazed to find that she could write in this vein. Had she changed?

The Clacton surgeon came downstairs and sat down to

have tea with me, the other doctor going off to another case. Mr. Percy Coleman was such a kind man and he asked if I had made any plans for my own future. I said that I had not, and he asked if I had a young man.

'Oh no,' I told him.

He was surprised. 'I should have thought that any girl with your face would have had a dozen,' he said. 'I don't like to think of you being so alone. If a young man did come along, take an old chap's advice, and think seriously about him.'

'No one will come along,' I ventured.

'You never know.' He finished his tea and then went to the waiting car. The last thing he said was, 'Don't forget that if a young man did come along, it might be the answer.'

Late that night when Mother was asleep, I walked out into the calmly beautiful moonlit night. It was always so lovely at Walton when the people were away and the beach was still. I wondered what the surgeon had really meant, then I knew that he was a kind man and he had not liked to think of me being so alone. It was good of him to think for me.

CHAPTER 8

Mother went back to the Radium Institute for further treatment, and this time I stayed behind, our funds were too low for both of us to go. I was nervously apprehensive of being alone, for Hertford House was capacious, and at any time the Zeppelins might be over.

I solved the difficulty the first two evenings by going to my room whilst it was still daylight, locking myself in and staying there. I did not think I could have faced the horror of going upstairs in the dark knowing nobody else was in the house with me, though not for the world would I have admitted that to Mother.

On the third morning I heard from Montie. He was passing through London expecting to be sent immediately out to India. He enclosed the money and a telegraph form, and asked if we could lunch. Would I meet him at Charing Cross, by the bookstall? On the spur of the moment I wired that I would, and caught the next train.

The whole of the journey I swung between the thrill of romantic adventure and the anguish that I was deceiving Mother. I ought not to be doing this, but I *was* doing it, and that in itself was exciting. I went to Charing Cross, walking into the station prepared to wait by the bookstall as he had said. Montie was there first. He was still good-looking, kindly and gentle, and looking much better in a second lieutenant's uniform than in that bulky fustian outfit which the privates wore. He had on a 'Gorblimey' cap which was the last word in smartness.

Both of us were on edge. We met like strangers, unsure of each other. We took a taxi to Brice's where we had lunched on 'treat' days at the time when I was living in St. Albans, and I was still excited though experiencing some mild emotional disappointment that the day was not as thrilling as I had expected.

We talked of London, of everybody being in uniform, and all the time there was a certain strained atmosphere that made itself felt. We lunched on shoddier food than previously, though we paid more for it, and we talked about the old times, avoiding the personal side. We knew that when he got to India, Montie would be fairly safe just as Joscelyn would be when he arrived in Egypt. He had brought me several of the cigarette cards I was collecting, flags of all nations series, and some very smart silk ones. I dared not confess that recently I had given up the idea and had handed mine on to a child who was interested. We discussed the Brides-in-the-Bath case; George Joseph Smith was due for execution next week.

We talked of 'The Glad Eye' and we paid one-and-six for the lunch, complaining about the expense. I was embarrassed that I was not more distressed to find how far apart we had gone. Montie must have realized this, for he said:

'You and I would never have made a go of it.'

'No, I suppose we shouldn't have done.'

I explained I wanted to get home before dark, so I should have to catch the afternoon train back.

'You always hated the dark,' he said. 'My word, remember that night the war broke out!' But he did not try to persuade me to stay.

I saw him off at Victoria, not on the verge of tears and quite surprised to recall that once I had sobbed my heart out for this man in that awful little waiting-room at Harpenden station. It was dreadful that now I did not even love him.

He brought me some white roses from the stall, there were no lilies-of-the-valley, and the roses reminded me of the frail white ones which grew just outside the schoolroom window when I was a child. It was for that memory that I wanted to cry, something far stronger than the thought of the man I once believed I loved and now had to admit that I hadn't.

I waved as the train chugged out, and I did hope that he would be safe, but all the time I knew that the prayer I prayed was only the one I would have prayed for a stranger, not for the man I wanted to marry. I'm all wrong, I thought, I've no heart, I'm not even sympathetic, but I hoped he would go to India and stay there out of harm's way. It didn't matter if we never met again.

Turning to walk down the platform to the barrier, I saw that, without my being aware of it, a train loaded with wounded from the front had come in on the other side. Stretchers were being borne past me. Men groaned. One of them was strapped to his stretcher and he screamed as if he had gone mad. It was a haunting sound which went all the way home with me. A stretcher was sprawled on the floor of the guard's van, two doctors beside it, apparently they were so intent on what they were doing that they did not realize I could see them. The man who lay there was very still, blood rose from his temple like a fountain rising straight up in a spiral. I had never imagined it could rise so high, and I tried not to look – yet still looked – and turned sick.

A dismal line of men marched past me clinging wounded to one another. They were young men who seemed to have shrunken into sudden age, their eyes still glazed with the horror of an endurance which I never saw in the Second World War.

'Now then, miss, now then,' said a couple of orderlies, carrying a stretcher past me. The man on the stretcher did not writhe or scream, and the sheet over him was taut. He had been young, but it was the young who died.

I drew aside, afraid, for it seemed horrible to be pushed away with a dead man so close, with the madman screaming, and that rising fountain of blood on the floor of the guard's van. I wanted to be sick.

Travelling back, I felt angry with the grown-up people, the diplomats, the M.P.s, and the men who should have seen this coming. Surely they could have protected the young? And they had let this happen. They were the ones who should have died, not these poor boys with the glazed eyes and that awfully *old* look about them. I cried in the train.

I got to Walton with the dusk, and the white roses fell to pieces in the road; somehow I did not fret for them. I got into the house and upstairs to my room before it was quite dark. Once it had become dark I should have been too afraid, something which I had always been ashamed to admit. I did not wait to get any supper, and was sorry about that later when I got hungry, but I had some water and half a bar of Fry's chocolate cream, which would do.

I began to think about the future. About Mr. Coleman and what he had said the afternoon of Mother's operation. About myself.

If Mother died my father would re-marry, I knew, and that would bar my return home. I was ashamed not to be able to tolerate my father's affections for other women, because I loved him in my own way, had once loved him deeply, but I did find it impossible to understand how he could behave like this. Nobody wanted to buy the stories I kept on writing, I did not know why I went on with them but somehow they were part of me and therefore undestroyable. They gave me happiness in their own way though I knew they would not sell. I felt so ill, so tired, and probably afraid of the future.

I knew that Mother hoped that I should marry before she died. *Before she died!* How horrifying that sounded! I realized that the knowledge of my security would at least bring her some light in the darkness of the final road, but I could see no future for either of us. Mother was waiting for a visitor on whom we could not close the door; not all the love or riches (had we had them) could thrust him away, for he was someone who would have to be met. I saw myself lost.

In the extravagant emotion of youth I was drenched in helplessness from which it seemed to be impossible to extricate myself, try as I would. I began to sob.

A maroon shot up into the night and I heard the 'Specials' rushing down the street, which always meant danger. I sat up in bed gripping my knees with my arms and staring at the locked door which I dared not open. I was half hysterical. At that moment I think I wanted to die more than I had ever done before. I wanted it to be now …

Joscelyn wrote from Gaza and we knew that he had reached a safe destination and if dysentery did not kill, him he would survive quite a long war in moderately comfortable surroundings. That was something, it meant he was secure. I never heard from Montie.

The trouble with this war was that there never seemed to be any sign of an end to it. In the beginning we had thought a mere handful of weeks would bring victory, then that phase passed, and now approaching the second winter we dared not ask questions. I thought we should never reach peace again. From the north the man who was ultimately to be my second husband wrote this:

> *Rosyth. October 1st, Thursday*
> Went ashore at three and played 15 holes at Dumfermline with Williams. Awful panic when I got back. Eight cyphers had come whilst I was ashore telling us to raise steam, and then cancelling it, and the Commander and I both being ashore the cypher couldn't be got at, so they had to go over to another ship to borrow one.

The Navy seemed to have its own experiences, and how in wartime the two gentlemen most concerned could slip ashore, I cannot imagine.

News of the death of Edith Cavell horrified us, I remember Mother was speechless. The Huns were loathsome, they did awful things and were indeed the beasts. I made the ghastly mistake of commenting that if Nurse Cavell was helping soldiers and sailors to escape, wasn't that espionage? I had to hold my tongue for the rest of the day. Of course I was shocked, with everybody else, but surely there was another side to it?

'If you say things like that everyone will think that we really are spies,' Mother told me with conviction. 'England will never forgive the Germans for this, and quite right, too! This is the sort of thing men do not forget.'

'Yes, of course,' I agreed.

We droned along in our rather dim life, keeping quiet because of the stigma we knew we had aroused, and doing nothing in particular. That autumn seemed to be a series of wretched events, but there was no sign of victory coming one inch nearer. There was the accident to King George the Fifth at the front, when his horse reared and he fell. An awful suspicion flowed everywhere that he had been killed by the enemy (one of those beastly spies, of course) and that the Press were just breaking it to us gently. In any emergency we all jumped to the conclusion that it must be a spy. A week later we knew that the King was still alive though badly injured.

On November the first Lewis Waller died, the 'flappers' delight' as he was known, and the hero of every young girl's passions. I wept privately, but dare not let Mother know in case she thought it ridiculous, but at Stratford-on-Avon I had hung round the idol of most of my girl friends. Now he was dead. I remember sitting in the window-seat of the sitting-room looking across the road to the grey sea and thinking 'this war will go on for ever'. Longing for young friends. For fun. For something gay, more than I was getting. And seeing no way out.

That was when my life changed.

CHAPTER 9

The Essex Cyclists manned their bicycles and pedalled away, some said to Burnham-on-Crouch but nobody knew for certain, and we had fond farewells. The officers were mostly married, and their young wives had provided something in the way of more youthful friends for me; one of their captains had for a time come round with chocolates, which were to provide my lunch and tea though he did not know that. He was nice, I remember his brown eyes were almost gold, and Mother let him take me out on the back of his motor-bike (my first effort in this direction), which in itself was an adventure.

The 24th Londons (the Queen's) immediately succeeded the Essex Cyclists. After the unfortunate affair of the rice pudding which the General had disliked, Arthur Denham-Cookes had settled down with the Queen's. He was a fair young man with grey-green eyes, not very tall but with that Blarney Stone charm that his Irish mother had given him.

We first met at the adjutant's dinner-party, somewhat disastrous for the fish pie was bad and the adjutant's wife burst into tears and said that she simply couldn't bear it. Afterwards we went into the drawing-room and had the entertainment fashionable at that period and known as an evening with music. Nito del Riego recited. He was extremely good-looking, and on all occasions was pushed to the front when entertainment was indicated. His sister Theresa had already published her beautiful song 'Oh, dry those tears'. I met her later, and she had great charm.

Arthur was Captain of the Day, so could not come to dine but arrived later armed to the teeth; he had just had to march to the end of Walton pier and back in the teeth of a gale. As the pier is second in length only to Southend that was indeed something.

He was to sing and asked for an accompanist, so I volunteered. He seemed doubtful of my ability, and later when I had done it, apologized for showing the doubt, asking if in return Mother and I would dine with him that week at the Albion Hotel where he was billeted. I said 'no', she said 'yes', so we went.

Everything in me warned me against that dinner. Yet really I should have loved it. Arthur was twenty-four, he spoke with a slightly Irish accent (mostly put on), and I sympathized with his deformed left hand which frequently made him shy, for he was secretly bitterly ashamed of it. He was young and I was sick for youth. He was rich, something to which I was unused, and he was gay.

'I'm a nice little fellow when you get to know me,' he confessed, 'but shy, so be kind to me.'

I met him next day in Walton High Street, when I was staring into a shop window, wondering if I could afford a *My Queen*, the speciality of the moment, but it had gone up to twopence.

'Buying the shop?' he asked.

'Oh no, nothing at the moment,' I said.

'Och, so the pin money's run out! Be damned to that,' and in he went.

I had never seen anybody buy chocolates like it. Even the local loony girl who ran the shop was cock-eyed with admiration. He bought three large boxes of this, four of that, said they were not large enough, then got the chauffeur to help me into the enormous open Sunbeam car he possessed and drive me home to Hertford House with him sitting beside me.

Within the week he took me to the regimental dance. Apparently he couldn't dance; the only time he had done, he had unhappily put his partner through some French windows, and as it was a first-floor room it was a trifle awkward. He did not seem too happy when I danced with Nito del Riego, so we sat out. He told me about his mother, who was something of a pest. His father had married again when seventy, an old gentleman with a fortune, and a daughter who was the first Lady Arthur Hill. His death had shattered his mother's nerves; privately he thought she was just a trifle dotty, but as it takes all sorts to make a world, who was he to complain?

'She's stone deaf amongst other things,' he said. 'Half my family are that way. She'd love to meet you. You must come up to London and meet her.'

'I wouldn't dare,' I confessed, paling visibly.

'Och but she'll love you,' said he. 'Don't let Ma worry you! She doesn't know how many blue peas make seven, never did. It's a mystery to me how I and my sister got born, but there you are.'

The last thing I wanted to do was to go up to London to meet a deaf lady who didn't know how many blue peas made seven, lived in glory in Prince's Gate, and might get the idea that her son was 'running after me'. However, the General came down to stay, now a Brigadier (that rice pudding scene must have been a very forceful one!), and he was the one who planned a jaunt.

The Brigadier gloried in a visit, much more so if somebody else was doing the paying. He thought we would all four go up and see the panto, and we could stay at Berners Hotel as Arthur's guests. We had no suitable clothes. There was one desperate winter's afternoon when I got out the sewing-machine which had made my sister's layette, and converted two frocks into something suitably 'evening', and did what was known in the family as one of my 'bodges'.

A week later we all started for London in the Sunbeam. I have to admit that any drive with Arthur at the wheel was a dramatic experience. Although the chauffeur drove part of the way, there came the moment when he didn't, after which we skidded through Stratford, and had one or two *contretemps* which I found most alarming (though I don't think they worried Arthur at all, for his principle always was that it took all sorts to make a world, so why worry?).

Berners Hotel was comfortable. Mother and I changed into the newly bodged clothes, felt pleased with ourselves, and went out to dine at the R.A.C. It was my first grown-up dinner, with any degree of smartness. Until this hour I had always been a little girl, it seemed. Mother called it *'backfisch'*, my father called it 'flapper'. Again, it takes all sorts to make a world.

We started with caviare, which bewildered me. I thought it was blackberries, and how you got blackberries in January was surely one of the seven wonders of the world. I was given champagne, which sent me dizzy for hours. Arthur was trying to arrange for us to lunch with his mother the next day, the last thing that I wanted, for Mother's coat looked shoddy and my cotton gloves were awful!

We went to a box at the theatre, again for the first time in my life; there were chocolates in packing the size of a baby's coffin, orchids to wear (another first time), and a 'Fums-up' doll which was the rage of that year.

'Look, he's got her a baby,' said the Brigadier, sparkling with champagne and thinking it an enormous joke, which mercifully I was too green to see.

During the evening something went wrong. Arthur telephoned home to make final arrangements with his mother and apparently she was in a rage. Lunch was off. He went quiet, had a stiff one, then got to the stage of explaining that he could not take us back to Walton in the car as he would not be returning for a couple of days. Mother said that was all right, we could go by train, and neither of us conveyed by a flicker of an eyelid that this horror would mean poverty for the rest of the month.

Much later in the year I knew that Arthur had told his mother he wanted to marry me and was 'bringing me round', and she had gone through the ceiling. It was an expensive ceiling too, at No. 6 Prince's Gate, painted like a springtime sky, but his mamma went through it with a bang. Who was I? How dare I? I must be an adventuress, and I must be low. The Denham-Cookes had the sort of set-up which had never entered my calm rectory, for although I believed that I knew something about bad tempers (my great-aunt Augusta was a lively lady who, if annoyed, would walk up to her knees in the local pond and scream that she would drown herself), I had yet to learn the free-fight-for-all moods into which this family could launch itself.

The evening ended deplorably, the Brigadier trying to carry things off well and entirely on my side, but we returned depressed.

Mother had seen in Arthur the security for the future of an adored daughter (one cannot blame her); she had recognized his attraction; and now something had happened to upset everything.

We jogged home in the slow train next day.

'We shall never see him round here again,' said Mother.

She was wrong.

Four evenings later the familiar ring came on the doorbell, and there he was with six dozen of the most expensive roses, and that provocative smile of his which one *had* to share.

'You thought you'd lost me,' said he, 'sure and that's a lie! "*Slanté* and *slanté* and *slanté* again," and have I and my ma had a row!'

In he came bubbling with joy.

We had a happy evening singing round the piano; he drank all the Three Gees we had in the place (Mother said young gentlemen of the aristocracy always did that), but it was satisfactory that the friendship was to continue.

The round of little parties, of dances, of Army concerts, with Nito persistently reciting 'If', went on. Then one foggy afternoon the chauffeur brought me a little note in Arthur's quite undecipherable handwriting. Never did a man write worse!

The Albion Hotel,
Walton-on-the-Naze.
January the 9th, 1916.

Dear Infant,

Can I come in this evening at eight? Don't have anyone else there, and don't say I'm coming, for it is a bit important.

Yours,

A.

It seemed odd that he should ask, usually he ran in and out just as he wished, but I had found moments when he behaved a little strangely, for he was unpredictable. It was a foggy night, and when I heard his ring I went to open the door. There he stood in full uniform with a Colt thrust into his belt, which meant that he was on duty.

'Why are you all dressed up like that?' I asked.

He grinned at me. A young sergeant was standing at the gate, a ghost figure in the fog. 'You wait for me, Sergeant,' Arthur said and stepped inside, closing the door after him. 'I'm Captain of the Day, that's all. It doesn't mean a thing.'

'Put the revolver down, won't you?'

'No, I've got to stay in the rig. Part of the duty. Fred Karno expects it of us. Got a drink?'

I poured it out for him, and he perched on the arm of the chesterfield sofa which Mother had bought at a bankrupt sale in Birmingham, so fulfilling a lifetime's ambition. He talked of Hertford House, how we had come by it, and did we like it? We did. It had been sheer luck that it had fallen into our hands. Houses interested him, he said, how many rooms had we?

The idea came to me that perhaps he had had a chat with the billeting officer and if we were billeted it would be an enormous help with the income. Only too anxious to put this forward I said that if he was interested in houses he could see over it. He would love it, he said, so we went up the curved staircase on to the first landing.

'It's dark on the next storey,' I said. 'We have not got proper curtains, and I dare not strike a light.'

'Sure!'

'They are such pretty views from the windows. You can see to the Oakleys across the backwater, and out to the Gunfleet in front.'

'But you don't look out much?'

'No, I'm busy,' I told him. I did not dare confess that we had no maid; those were the days when only the low-downs did without, so we had invented a fictitious maid called Emily, who was always having a night off at convenient moments, or hadn't heard the bell, or something of that kind. Emily lived only in our imagination of course, but to the rest of the world she was a very real person, so we hoped.

Curiously enough Arthur wanted to go to the top floor which I thought was extraordinary. I was worried about the lights showing and another row coming with the 'Specials'; anyway tonight in the fog he'd see nothing. He went alone, was gone some time groping his way about, and now I got the strange feeling that something was wrong. Once the idea came I could not dismiss it, so when he came down, I challenged him.

'Are you going to billet us?'

'Not on your life! They never billet when there isn't a man in the house. I'm not up to any harm. I'm a nice little fellow when you get to know me.'

We went downstairs again, and paused by the dining-room door. 'I haven't seen the kitchen,' he said.

'Goodness, you *do* want to see a lot!'

We went into the kitchen, with the stone step dropping down on to its bricked floor which was so difficult to keep clean. Frank, the cat (he turned out to be a girl after that, proving it in the most obvious manner), was sitting by the door waiting to go out. I picked the cat up and had my hand on the latch, but Arthur stopped me.

'Don't go out. You mustn't go out.'

'Why not? The cat wants to go out.'

'All right. I'll do it.' He went to the nasty little window over the sink and rapped on it, instantly a man spoke. The man must have been in our back-yard, which was something of a surprise. 'All right, Sergeant,' Arthur said, then slipped the cat out.

'What is all this?' I asked.

'I can't tell you. I will one day, but for the moment you've got to trust me.'

'Who is that outside?'

'Nobody to worry you if you do as I tell you. Let's go back to Mummy.'

We went back, I feeling most uncomfortable, and I seemed to have infected Arthur with this, for he refused a drink, and said he would have to be back on duty. We went into the hall, and he picked up his 'British Warm' off the chair. Perhaps he knew that I was worried, for he turned to me.

'Believe me, I'm on your side in this,' he said, and at the door he called to the man beyond it. 'Sergeant Bryant?'

'Yes, sir?'

As he opened that door I realized for the first time that the house had been surrounded. 'What are those men doing here?' I asked.

Without a word he turned, saluted, then marched away, the men with him. I went back to Mother, my knees shaky. It all seemed to be so absurd. 'What do you suppose it was?' I asked her.

Neither of us guessed the truth. It was only after we were married that I found it. The story of our being spies had gone further and orders had come to Colonel Concannon. The Army were tightening up against the spy menace. I think the Colonel, knowing us, was sorry, but had to take action, so he sent the one officer who he knew would treat us well. An armed picket had surrounded Hertford House, and inside it to fulfil his duty Arthur had gone into every room. In reality he had looked at nothing, but had done what he was told and was petunia with rage.

The spy story went on. All the time we were being watched. The worst part of all was that there was not a thing we could do about it.

It was a gayer spring than the others if only because young people came in and out of the house. There were the subs. – Fred Goosey, young Bushell and Nito del Riego; there were concerts, soldiers' theatricals, dances, and dinners. It was now for the first time that I realized I was one of those unfortunate girls who had side-stepped adolescence. I had grown up completely on the day my mother left my father, and I had recognized it was my duty to see after her. But at this hour I grew younger.

The affair with Arthur was not progressing. I found him a charming friend, loved his music, and sympathized with his rather pathetic loneliness. The hand worried him so much.

'It's awfully silly to get so upset about it,' I said. 'People don't really notice.'

'Don't they just! Half the stupid old women who would have given me white feathers without it, treat it as an honourable war scar.'

'Why not pretend it is?'

In a sudden rush of confidence he said: 'When I was a kid, Ma always made me sit on it so that people wouldn't see. She felt pretty sticky about it, too. The first thing the Governor said when he saw me was, "Well, there's one boy who will never go into the Army." '

'That shows how much he knew!' I told him. 'Look at you now!'

'You can't call this the Army, it's Fred Karno's whatnot. The Guards had me out damned quick when they spotted it. I'd have the devil of a job to get overseas.'

'Aren't you lucky!'

'Lucky? Hell!' and he went scarlet. 'I don't want other fellows to die for me, I want to do my bit. Think I like this? If you do, think again.'

He had pluck all right, but he still went on feeling badly about the hand, and the three false fingers that he wore on it, covered by a tiny worsted mitten.

'Makes you feel sick, doesn't it?' he asked.

'No, it doesn't. Why should it?'

'Thanks a lot for that, *acushla*,' he said tenderly.

There was another bad night when the Zepps came over at the end of March, the night when Joachim Breithaupt was brought down at Rainham, and that was something, for he had been captain of Zepp L15, which had done so much harm on London last autumn. The Zepps were hanging about half the night, it seemed, and one of the soldiers in them must have looked out over our backwater behind Hertford House, for next morning there was a German cap lying on the mud. One of the Queen's men found it, and sold it for five bob to an officer in the 23rd Londons then stationed in Frinton. It was a man of Arthur's company, and he charged in for a drink at eleven, red with fury.

'Sold it to the 23rds! Can you beat it! It ought to be a trophy of the regiment, and what does he do, picks it up and all for a wretched five bob trots it over to Frinton and sells it to the first chap who makes a bid for it!'

'Buy it back?' suggested Mother.

'Do you think I haven't tried? Och, but I was over there and after the chap, it's Captain Harris who has it; I offered him a fiver, and he just waggled it at me and said all the tea in China wouldn't get it out of him. It makes me livid.'

The papers said that ninety bombs had been dropped in the eastern counties, certainly it had sounded like it.

It seemed sickening that this particular spring we had none of the thrill of a big push coming. Last year we had been so certain, but this year we were droning along with nothing much happening, and peace no nearer.

The idea of any sudden spurt and the war smashing out in a single conflict was dead, but the *Daily Mail* of April the second was depressing.

There was a beastly article in it, 'The End is Not Near. Spring prospects of the war', by Lovat Fraser. It ended with:

> The ultimate victory of the Allies seems more certain and inevitable than it was a year ago, but there is not one sure or safe sign that the war is anywhere near a close.

'Well,' said Mother, 'all I can say to that is that it is a good thing that a year ago we did not know how sticky was our wicket. We at least have that to be thankful for.'

Lots more barbed-wire entanglements were going on to the cliffs, and loads of sandbags kept coming up. A special company had gone out to Holland Gat at the far end of the Frinton golf links, which it was said was dangerous, for there in the 1910 manoeuvres it had been proved that the water was of sufficient depth for a fleet to come close, bombard, and perhaps land. That was a nice thing!

It's thrilling, I thought. It's exciting. I wouldn't have missed it for the world, and if only Mother were better some of it would be rather fun.

At that hour I had not realized that at the very beginning of the war, Dover had been submitted to an ordeal which could very easily come our way given time. In October 1914 every home in Dover had been served with this notice:

> The inhabitants of Dover are informed that they are to evacuate the town *immediately.* All civilians resident in the district described on the enclosed sheet must meet at the place of assembly at — and there await orders to leave for the country together on foot. Vehicles will, as far as possible, be provided for those unable to walk. Each person must carry warm clothing and food and drink for twelve hours.
>
> Mr. A. C. Leney will act as Evacuating Officer, with headquarters at the Town Hall.
>
> .... Mayor.

I was young enough and silly enough to think that if there was an evacuation it would be something to have seen and done, and of course it would all turn out all right in the end. I had a blind faith in the mercy of providence.

'If anything like that happens, I shan't wait for wagons to get me out,' said one of the subs. 'The first bicycle I can pinch, I'll pinch, and hop it with amnesia. That ought to excuse me.'

That week my mother wrote to my father:

Hertford House,
Walton-on-the-Naze.
April the 8th, 1916

Dear Harvey,

The bombs have been bad all round us. Some were dropped on the munition works at Stowmarket and did a good deal of harm, and the sound of the reports shook us up. The same day a ship struck a mine just off Walton, and I thought the house would come down. We have a great many wounded soldiers here now, they march past very slowly every morning and are then dismissed for the day. Some of the French are with them, and it is very interesting.

We have not heard from Joscelyn for a long time, and when he wrote he complained that he had had no regular letters from us, though we do write regularly.

Ursula sends her love.

MARY

The French wounded caused a casualty in our home, for I had a tortoise by the name of Daniel who browsed in the front garden. The soldiers found they could whistle him up, as he was very tame and came out if called. (He ate chocolate.) One of the Frenchies threw a ship's biscuit at him, and poor Daniel had his head out and was killed. I was indignant about it and Arthur said he would get me another, then found he couldn't, for tortoises were not being imported during the war, and the man whom he asked about it was rude.

Arthur was very angry, but angrier about Mr. McKenna's Budget. Cocoa, sugar, and coffee would be dearer, not that any of those bothered him, but there was a trebled duty on the rich man's car. The lowest income tax was to be two-and-three, and the highest eight-and-six. He was in the eight-and-six class.

'I would be!' he said, 'and if you ask me they aren't getting on with the war. We are taxed to the hilt, it gets us nowhere, and everybody is hanging about waiting for something to happen. What a world!'

Mr. McKenna's new ruling had given his ma a heart attack. He laughed about it, which I thought rather hard on her. I was getting an odd picture of this very beautiful but possessive lady, who had been an old man's darling, and now lived in an enormous mansion where she was admirably protected by Old Rowland her personal maid (a bulldog, I gathered), Old Jim, who had once been the children's nanny, but had never pushed a pram in her life because it was demeaning and the duty of an under-nurse only, and Chown the butler who was a pet.

But none of these could protect Ma from the Zepps, and she went night after night into the cellar, in what Arthur said she would have termed 'unsuitable attire', and sat there heroically until the danger passed by. Arthur was casual about her difficulties.

'Bombs never fall in the right place,' said he. 'Only the other night my three uncles and my cousin were in Uncle Billy's place, when a bomb took the area railings. Had it removed all of them I should have been Lord Lurgan, and that would have been an occasion! Och, but it makes you sick!'

'Too bad!' I murmured.

He brought amusement into my life. He was such fun, and I was growing fonder of him. I felt that had he really wanted me he would have asked at Christmas, but that occasion had gone wrong on us. What had I done? I still did not know.

The April weather was mild, and it was nice that the primroses had come. All the soldiers seemed to be very busy, we had an idea that something was on though we dare not mention it, and we had fewer musical evenings in consequence.

I went out to the shops, met Arthur on a bicycle, and he seemed to be in a disturbed mood, and hardly stayed to speak to me. I imagined his mother had been difficult again, for by now I had become accustomed to the fact that he was quite under her thumb, and she had only to start a row to reduce him to a frazzle. It was, I thought, the usual maternal argument.

On my return home Mother met me. She was standing in the hall with a piece of paper in her hand. 'Here it is,' she said and held it out to me. I read it.

> All civilians resident in the district described on the enclosed sheet must meet at the place of assembly at Walton church, and there await orders to leave for the country together on foot. Vehicles will, as far as possible, be provided for those unable to walk. Each person must carry warm clothing, and food and drink for twelve hours …

It was signed Stanley Nicholson, Clerk to the Council.

My first feeling was one of supreme thrill. 'Good gracious!' I said. 'Isn't that exciting?'

Mother, her face like a mask, said, 'Isn't it?' No more.

I read on about the ringing of the church bell which

must be accepted as the warning, and when that came the town must be evacuated *immediately*. Reading this, I got the feeling that my two feet were no longer on mother earth. 'What happens to the house and the furniture?' I asked.

'Oh, I expect they'll be all right,' Mother said, and I was so elated that I did not realize she was being unnaturally calm. To me it was one of the most exciting things that had ever happened, and eagerly I prepared to get things ready. Two blankets. Iron rations. Could we take our famous Tommy's cooker as well? I began to wonder if my old osteomyelitis ankle would hold up to any long march, comforting myself with the assurance that anyway it would have to, and it was quite a good time of the year for a nice long walk. Mother would be all right in a wagon, and that was what mattered most. Never did it occur to me that our evacuation from Walton would be anything but the greatest fun, and something to talk about for years!

I ran out to Mr. Mills the grocer for a tin of bully beef for the trip and he told me that he understood that as the civilians went inland along the peninsula to Colchester we should be quite safe, for their garrison would be coming out into action to defend Frinton and Walton. I never realized that our departure would be hurried by German shells from the sea, and the outcoming troops would have been an additional trial on the narrow roads. At the time I was gay about it, exuberant if anything, for this showed that we were getting on with the war, weren't we? It was rumoured that Cambridge was our destination. Some walk!

The imminence of invasion seemed to increase, so much so that we no longer dared to undress at night in case we should be caught unawares, which would be most improper. (In 1916, the thought of anybody ever seeing me in my stalwart cambric nightdress with my hair down, sent me into a tizzy!)

My own letter to my father at the time explains it.

Hertford House,
Walton-on-the-Naze.
April the 24th. Monday.

Dear Dad,

We have only been to bed in our clothes and the guns began heavily at sea early this morning. Invasion is expected before Tuesday night, and the troops are coming in, it would almost seem in their thousands. A thousand of the Essex Cyclists camped by the roadside outside Walton last night, and a large number of the Yeomanry were camping behind them. Of course it may only be a big scare, but all yesterday they were at work fortifying the place and the big men from the War Office were down here, so it looks quite serious. The troops are up day and night, and you can't get in or out of the place without passes.

Love from

URSULA

In that same hour a young sub-lieutenant wrote in his diary this message:

Sea – Scapa. April 24th, 1916
Awful panic. Last night we were suddenly ordered by the C.-in-C. to take a new route to Scapa and come in by the Pentland Firth, close to where the *King Edward* lies anchored in Scapa. Arrived at 1.30 p.m. and took in 970 tons of coal, taking about 6 hours over it.

Scapa-Kirkwall. April 25th, 1916
Got under way at 6a.m. and came round to Kirkwall, where we are apparently going to lie

> for some time. Some German ships came over and bombarded Lowestoft at an early hour this morning, with any luck they were caught on the way back.

On our hall chair two folded blankets rested, a tin of bully, a packet of biscuits, and a bottle of water, but we didn't evacuate on the Tuesday.

'If they stay there long we'll be sick to death of the sight of them,' said Mother.

'Do you think it'll happen?' I asked her.

'Probably. If you put yourself in the Huns' place what would you do? Invade if you could.'

'I suppose so,' I agreed.

In spite of the shelling of Lowestoft, the scare of invasion seemed to wear itself out a little. Suddenly the passes were cancelled, and we could go in and out of Walton again, though nobody could get anywhere near Harwich or the Oakleys. It was said that they were making high explosives on Bramwell Island, which lay at the head of the backwater, and at times there were explosions and rumours of people being blown up. If I had not been under the suspicion of being a spy I should have gone exploring on my ancient B.S.A. bicycle ('Made-like-a-Gun', one of our favourite Britons-never-never-never-shall-be-slaves slogans) of which I was enormously proud. But things being as they were I daren't go.

Arthur came round and said thank goodness things were easing off, and what a time it had been, but that was all we were told of it.

'It really is the most wonderful epoch in which to live,' said Mother. 'I wish we knew more about it, but I suppose today all the interesting bits have to be kept highly secret.'

Arthur came in most nights. He had a habit of drinking neat whisky, which was a dreadful tax on our resources, and he was the only man I had ever seen do this.

'Doesn't it taste awful?' I asked him.

'Sure, and it does! But afterwards you feel like a giant, nothing matters at all, at all.'

He was slight, very thin, rather frail if he had spoken the truth about himself, and I don't suppose he often felt like a giant. We celebrated the fact that things had cooled down, had an evening round the piano, and the blankets and iron rations having gone out of the hall we felt comforted.

'But we missed something awfully exciting,' I told Arthur, wondering what the walk with covered wagons would have been.

'You're an awful little goose!' he said gaily.

Mother's condition kept worsening. I had until now been trying to buoy myself up with the silly pretences one adopts in self-defence. Perhaps the doctors were wrong; perhaps a miracle cure would come out in time; perhaps something – anything – would happen. The pain was worrying her now, and when the doctor came he gave me a box of tablets for her.

'She can have one to sleep on, but you must be careful. She can never have more than two.'

'Are they dangerous?'

He stood there fiddling with a bowler hat in the hall, one of those bluff little men who call a spade a spade. 'Oh yes, m'dear, three would be tricky, four could be the end. You can't joke with these things, but you're a sensible girl.'

'Yes,' I said.

Whilst she slept that afternoon I sat on the beach and thought about it. I hate suffering. I stared out to the Gunfleet sands knowing full well that what I contemplated would be mortal sin. Mortal sin is something of which I have a horror, early training did that. But I would face it for Mother. It could not be wicked to help someone I loved so that she suffered less. I took six of the tablets out of their box.

I locked these carefully away into a little doll's wardrobe that I cherished with fond memories of my 'doll' days. In it I treasured four of my first teeth (heaven only knows why), the tiny gold cross I wore for my confirmation, a ring Mother gave me but which could not be worn until I was 'of age', as she disliked girls wearing rings, and the mosaic brooch Montie had given me when he went with the Fire Brigade to Turin.

To this collection I had added six tablets.

I've got to do it, I told myself as I sat on the beach. Then I thought that a German shell might destroy both of us before I sought to destroy one of us.

A young soldier came by, paused, his face flushed, his eyes admiring. 'Penny for your thoughts, miss,' he said.

That was something I couldn't have told him.

CHAPTER 10

It was a hot eleventh of May and during the morning Arthur came round.

'Are you and Mummy doing anything this evening?'

'Absolutely nothing. Why?'

'I want to have a talk with Mummy.'

'What about?'

'Ask no questions and you'll be told no flibberty-gibbets. No, honest as they come, I want to talk to Mummy. If I come in after dinner will that be all right?'

'I'll tell her.'

'And I want no infants hanging around.'

'Meaning me?'

'Meaning you,' he said, and laughed, then off he went again. He had not even had a drink.

I thought it was queer, and Mother was afraid that he might have heard something about our being spies, and prayed it was no further trouble on that score. I let him in when he came, then went to the little dining-room to talk to our fictitious maid-servant Emily, whilst he and Mother were in the sitting-room. I sat on the table edge and was apprehensive.

Supposing Arthur was asking Mother about marrying me? He had very old-fashioned ideas in some ways, and this was just the sort of thing that he would do. I did not want to marry. Mother hated the thought of leaving me alone in the world, and nothing would comfort her more than to know I was with him, I realized that, but what do I *do*? I asked myself.

Arthur had considerable charm, but was a changeable personality, at moments gauche, at others warmly amusing. His gaiety was infectious and a tonic to me, but suddenly this night I was afraid of him.

Mother came into the dining-room looking utterly delighted, which she had not looked for months now. The change in her spurred me on. 'He wants to speak to you, darling,' then impulsively: 'Ursula, I am so happy, so very, very happy. I am just so happy.'

Arthur was sitting on the sofa looking radiant too, his face flushed, his eyes grey-green and dancing. 'I suppose you know what all this is about?' he asked.

'I'm not sure.'

'I'd be an awfully nice little fellow to marry.'

'Would you now?'

He changed at that. 'Darling infant, I know you aren't in love with me, but I've got enough love for both of us, and I'll give you the lot. Lands and proud dwellings and all that stuff, and a coronet, Zillah, thy brow shall entwine. I want to marry you most awfully.'

'Why?'

'Because you are the nicest girl I have ever met.' He began to giggle. 'What d'you think happened when I told Ma about it?'

'I should think she had a fit.'

He began to sing:

'And when I told them
How wonderful you are,

They didn't believe me,
They didn't believe me.

That was what happened, infant! Ma said awful things and then I said worse. It was one big hell of a row but now I've won the day. Darling, it *is* going to be "yes"?'

'I suppose so,' I said.

Afterwards I realized that it was hardly the most enthusiastic acceptance, and he always said, 'She never wanted to marry me, but I made her.'

In exuberance he tore back to the Albion and returned in the Sunbeam with a couple of bottles of champagne. He and Mother did well on it, and I had a teaspoonful 'for luck', which sent me dizzy to bed.

I had become engaged to a rich young man who could see after me for ever. I had made Mother so happy that tonight her old smile had returned, and she seemed to have forgotten the pain. Mother *was* happy, yet I didn't sleep at all that night.

Being engaged to Arthur was unbelievable.

The whole world changed, and he himself was amusing in his joy. He rushed the announcements into the papers before Ma started to make a fuss, or the Germans landed, or something ridiculous happened. He got sudden leave, which the Colonel did not want to give him, and dashed up to London, having one car accident at Romford, and another in Chelmsford on the return journey.

He had wired the Brigadier who was one of those dapper elderly gentlemen who adore a social jaunt. He prided himself on being something of a 'picker' when it came to spending, and there was nothing he liked better than dipping into somebody else's purse. Meeting at the R.A.C. they went on to Marshall's, and there made friends with the model dress buyer, a Miss Parker, so they said. They were set on two small gilt chairs, and dresses were displayed for them. They bought three, some lingerie, and an evening cloak, the Brigadier fixed up a dinner engagement with Miss Parker, and on they went to Bond Street.

There they bought a sapphire and diamond engagement ring, and a bracelet to go with it. A string of pearls, and a small gold mesh bag (highly fashionable at the time), little realizing that I had not two-and-eightpence in the world to put inside it.

'Whatever happens he must never know how hard-up we are,' Mother explained.

'Of course not.'

These exciting parcels were sheer ecstasy, and then we went back to the Albion to chicken and champagne with him. At that moment the chicken was far more use to me than the diamonds, sapphires, and pearls. I'll never know myself all dressed up like that, I thought.

Next day he was back with five pounds' worth of flowers. I thought the chauffeur would never stop carrying them in. The following morning it was chocolates. Then we had a serious talk. I told him he must not give me so much, I had no intention of ruining him, and it must stop, right now! I showed him innumerable letters from photographers, dressmakers, florists and such, to do with my wedding.

'Nothing from Ma?' he asked.

There was indeed nothing from Ma. He went back to the Albion and telephoned her; I gathered the conversation was not satisfactory. She was so deaf that she had to leave interpretation to Rowland, her personal maid, and Rowland was not an interpreter of the first-class variety. Arthur decided that he would go up and see her, and drove half the night, returning in a fury at dawn. Next time, he said, he'd take his Colt with him, and shoot both Ma and Rowland. 'Women!' said he. 'Oh, my God! Women!'

'What's the matter?' I had got him into our sitting-room and the truth came out. Mrs. Denham-Cookes had discovered that Mother was living away from my father, and she wanted this to end, otherwise she would never agree to the wedding. As I listened I went cold.

'Look here,' I said, 'if anybody is going to get at my mother, this affair ends right now.'

'Darling, you couldn't let me down?'

'I could,' and he knew that I meant it! I would not marry him at all if he made any pass at trying to persuade Mother to return to the rectory.

He got up. 'Right,' said he. 'Now there is nothing left for it but to go up to Prince's Gate and shoot Ma. I shall swing for this, but at least I'll have done something.'

He got the better of the second row, and came back in a burst of success. A week later I went with him to pay my first visit to Prince's Gate.

As we entered the big hall, Mrs. Denham-Cookes was coming down the stairs, and she was one of the most beautiful women that I have ever seen. Both of us were nervous, as we went into the library which looked out on the almost countrified gardens behind the great house. Her ear trumpet was alarming. We talked banalities. Where had I been to school? I hadn't. When did I come out? I never had. When was I presented? With the same answer. My future sister-in-law sat by, and I could not eat my tea; we left early, Arthur red with rage.

'But she's seen me, surely that's something? Did she say anything to you about me?'

'Only that you had very beautiful eyes.'

We nearly missed the train and when we got back to Walton it was obvious that something exciting was afoot. It was a good deal more exciting than we knew.

The German Fleet was out.

Extra guards had been set along the front, and fresh troops were pouring in so that the road to Colchester was almost blocked again. At Hertford House a couple of blankets were back in the hall, and the iron rations tucked into the old string bag.

'I shouldn't have come back,' said Arthur. 'What a shemozzle this is going to be!'

At that very hour a young sub-lieutenant, who never comes into this book but who only a handful of years later came into my life for keeps, wrote this:

> *May 31st*, 1916. *Swin – Sea – Black Deep*
> Sub-Calibre all the forenoon. Raised steam for full speed with the utmost despatch in the afternoon and rushed out. We cleared ship for action, and really thought we were in for something. However, we anchored at 6.30 at the southern end of the Black Deep, in the middle of the North Sea and a prey to submarines.
>
> *June 1st. Black Deep – Sea – Swin*
> Got up anchor at 2 p.m. and came back to the Swin, coaling on arrival. Awful panic tonight, and there has apparently been a Fleet action of sorts which we of course missed. *The Marlborough* is flooded up to the main deck, and the *Warspite* has gone into dock, and the C.-in-C. is signalling everywhere for hospital ships. We were apparently kept south in case the Germans detached a raiding squadron.
>
> *June 3nd. Swin – Sheerness*
> Came back to Sheerness after lunch. From what I can gather the action yesterday was quite a big affair, in which we don't seem by any means to have got the best of it. (Awful bad luck being out of it after waiting eighteen months!)

That was the attitude of the morning papers after the Battle of Jutland, due to the fact that the Admiralty had revealed our losses but not those of the Germans.

'Anyway, God bless the Navy,' said Mother.

Almost immediately after that, disaster came. On June the fifth Lord Kitchener set off for Archangel in H.M.S. *Hampshire*,, and he and nearly all the ship's company went down never to be heard of again.

'There was a spy on board,' said everyone, '*of course* there was a spy on board. That's sticking out a mile.'

Although we were getting used to dramatic horrors, none of us had thought of Lord Kitchener being killed, and all the older people despaired. They said we couldn't win the war without him. We younger ones thought new blood was a good idea.

'How foolish you children are!' said the older and wiser ones. 'That would be disastrous.'

Mr. Lloyd George became Secretary of State for War and the gossips said he would soon be Prime Minister. The blankets and the iron rations popped back into the cupboard, but of course they would be out again sooner or later.

The Victoria Cross was won for the first time on our own soil when Lieutenant Leefe Robinson brought down a Zepp in flames at Cuffley.

'This is triumph,' said Mother, even if she didn't like aeroplanes. 'We'll win the war after all.'

I don't know where she got that idea! I could see no immediate hope ahead, and on the home front the food prices were shooting up and horrifying me. The bread was so difficult. Chocolates were growing scarcer and those we could get had a new taste about them which had never been there before. 'Three Gees' was now four-and-threepence a bottle and I was absorbed in the complexities of making-do.

Early in August Mother wrote to my father.

Hertford House,
Walton-on-the-Naze.
August the fourth, 1916

Dear Harvey,

Things are getting much more difficult here, for we cannot get either a woman or a child to help us, and I am very helpless, whilst Ursula's health has been so bad. I feel it is hopeless to go on as we are doing. Arthur complains that Ursula has no right to do the washing-up, which is true.

It is a worrying time for all of us, but what can we do? Ursula is ill; she gets so depressed and unhappy. The poor child is very much thinner, which worries me.

As ever,

MARY

If I had inherited much of my mother's spirit of determination, the background of the war was in itself undermining. Also I was worried about Arthur. In many ways I found him unpredictable. Charmingly gay, amusing, and generous, yet there were things about him which I did not understand. One of his brother officers, a widower and a man I had liked very much, tried to persuade me to break off the engagement.

'But why?' I asked.

'Because I like you very much. I want to see you happy, truly happy, I mean.'

'I am happy,' I told him.

Arthur was perhaps unpredictable because he was as ever having trouble with Ma; she wanted this, she wanted that, and the truth of the whole matter was that she *didn't* want him to marry. Although he had a couple of thousand a year of his own, his Army pay, and those dainty details known as 'perks' which went with it, her extra substantial allowance buttered his bread. Nothing would persuade him to forgo that. 'It would be living in stinking poverty, and I'm not good at all, at all at that sort of thing,' he said.

On August the twenty-fifth Mother wrote again to my father and her letter gives a curious insight into a condition of that war, which people in the Second World War believed to be peculiar only to them.

Hertford House,
Walton-on-the-Naze.
August the 25th, 1916

Dear Harvey,

I go to the Radium Institute at ten o'clock on Monday the fourth of September, and shall be there every day until 4 p.m. so I hope you will be able to come and see me there. I *particularly* want to see you. The Institute is in Riding House Street close to the Langham Church, Langham Place, you should have no difficulty in finding it. Let me know which days you will be up. I am not up to much today, as the Zepps were awful in the night, two bombs dropped close to this house, but fortunately neither of them exploded; we heard and saw about 80 dropped; they were over Harwich again, and the Zepps went over this house rather low, the engines being very noisy.

As soon as we hear them coming we put on dressing-gowns and sit in the front garden, then we can see them and feel safer than in the house.

Today there has been incessant firing at sea, very very heavy, and we expect Zepps tonight as they generally favour us with two nights in succession, and it is foggy. But Arthur will come round if there are any more tonight, and we have gas masks, etc. to prevent feeling the fumes, but it is very weird when they are about as we muddle round in the dark.

Please write as soon as you can and say when you are coming. Ursula is better today, but the doctor says these alarms upset her, though London is worse to be in, I imagine.

Yours affectionately,

MARY

(I have no recollection of being served with gas masks, and think these must have been something Arthur obtained for us, though I had no idea there were any in England at the time.)

The Queen's were moved to Frinton, and the Worcesters and Gloucesters came in their place. The change was unexpected, but somehow or other Arthur got himself 'lent' to the Worcesters and Gloucesters, with the most disastrous result.

He had been with them but four days when his batman appeared, very pink in the face, with a note for me. It had been written in a hurry, telling me that there had been some ghastly misunderstanding which it was impossible to explain, but his Sam Browne had been removed, and he was now under arrest. He had not a clue what it was all about, he'd done nothing, but would I go to the telephone, ring up the Brigadier and ask for help?

Privately I was afraid of the Brigadier, whom I always felt I should address as 'Sir', and I did not like this job, but I undertook it. The Brigadier was at home, and he received the information in a manner most martial, told me he would be with us shortly, and banged down the receiver.

'I only hope he doesn't think he is going to stay in this house,' said Mother, aghast at the prospect.

'Oh no. He'd go to the Marine or the Albion, surely? If he tries, we'll tell him that Emily has left,' I said.

It was evening when the Brigadier walked in in a

commanding manner, and with the air that only one who has served with the Madras Pioneers could produce. Everything was under control, above-board and ship-shape. He had interviewed the Colonel, who he thought was mad; he had insisted that Arthur was immediately released, which command had been complied with. He'd be along soon, and would tonight return to the Queen's. I could not quite fathom what had happened, but Mother said that it was bound to be all right if the Brigadier had taken such action, and the thing to do was not to ask too much. It was a man's war, anyway, and nothing to do with us.

But I was dubious. It all seemed rather queer.

We arranged to marry in the November.

At this time my father appeared to have drifted apart from me. As a child I had been deeply devoted to both my parents, but now, over-sympathetic with my mother, I felt that he had not helped us as he might over the trouble about our being spies. I very much resented the fact that another woman, now living at the rectory, would be awaiting my mother's death, which could not be far off. Yet over my coming marriage my father behaved with great generosity, for after discussing my marriage settlement with Arthur he settled £800 on me, which was almost everything he had. He came down to see us about this, a rather unhappy visit, with stormy autumn weather, and all of us gauche with one another, for the old friendliness was dead.

Food problems were again besetting us. In London Tuesdays were to be meatless days, whilst in the country Wednesday was the allotment. There was a shortage of potatoes, so that we had five potatoless days, which was difficult, for the bread had become most unpleasant, and there was really nothing to eat as a vegetable save mangolds, turnips, and such.

But on October the first *The Bing Boys* came to London, and Arthur rushed up to see it, and promised to take me later. George Robey was wonderful, Vi Loraine a joy, and within twenty-four hours all London was singing:

If you were the only girl in the world,
And I was the only boy.

I went up one day to see Mrs. Denham-Cookes, who had commanded the visit. Wedding presents were pouring into the house at Walton, and she gave me a ruby crescent brooch, whilst my sister-in-law, who could have had no imagination (or, as my brother commented, 'too much'), gave me a silver mustard-pot! Visits to Prince's Gate were uncomfortable, the only person I could like there being the butler, who was a darling, but I hardly dared say that in case it emphasized my commonness.

We were arranging to take a furnished house in Frinton, and to give up Hertford House, which would be too much for Mother. She was to live at The Cedars on the front (then a boarding-house) about twenty houses from Thalassa, which I took.

Arthur had sent me over to get a suitable house, his instructions being that it must be better than the Colonel's and to hell with the cost! The agent telling me that Thalassa would be billeted if I did not take it, and that the landlord was in a tizzy over this, I offered thirty shillings a week, and to my own huge surprise, got it. It had ten bedrooms, three sitting-rooms, a huge lounge hall, with spacious garden, and faced the greensward.

Arthur was disappointed that it was cheap, for his mother said that anything cheap was common, so that I felt crushed. I engaged a cook, Mrs. Fanthorpe, a parlourmaid, a housemaid, a tweeny. Arthur's batman would help, and his old manservant who was in the regiment would come to us as butler. Then he insisted that I must have a personal maid, because Ma had one. I engaged a genteel creature of whom I was afraid, and was dubious of the success of this venture, and how correct I was!

So I made all the preparations to become rich.

We were to be married at Frinton church, and the reception was to be at the Beach House Hotel. Mother and I were being flung into multitudinous expenses that we could not afford, yet determined to give the right impression. My wedding dress was five pounds (mercifully I did not realize how inferior it was), and I had made all my own lingerie with Mother's help, but neither of us would have admitted this, in case we lost prestige, for in those days it was not clever to do things oneself.

We pretended to be what is euphemistically known as 'comfortably off'. We made our plans, trying to conceal the fact that we were attempting the impossible, and the night before my marriage we gave a party at the Marine Hotel.

That afternoon I went to the local pawnshop, and pawned the little silver brushes and boxes which I had collected from childhood. With the money I went to kind old Mr. Barker at the Marine and explained that I wanted to pay for the party myself, and he was to tell Mother only when she came to pay the day after tomorrow. He was very sweet, he looked at me with gentle eyes, I think he guessed how poor I was, but he said nothing.

Mother and I walked to the hotel that evening, both of us praying that the morrow, my wedding day, would be a 'good day', the unhappy phrase which is forced on the fatally sick.

The night was fair.

There was the familiar scent of tamarisk and brine, and we spoke little, but that was the last time when we should ever be really alone with each other in the dear old fond relationship. In that few minutes' walk we came closer than ever again in the few weeks that were left to her. The sea beat against the stone wall and searchlights swept the sky. To me it seemed that we parted for ever as we entered the Marine that night.

I have always thought of it that way.

CHAPTER 11

The wedding day was dense with fog and melancholy with foghorns coming from the sea. But it *was* a 'good day' for Mother. The personal maid who had arrived last night was already making her presence felt in a house which was vainly trying to conceal the narrowness of its means from her. It was with some agility that I got down at six to set her breakfast, pretending that 'the woman' had been in! It was maddening that she did not like eggs and was fussy about her toast.

She then wished to press the wedding dress and did not like the kitchen table. The morning was beset with worries.

My father arrived at eleven in considerable agitation because his suit had been put by for some years and, growing stouter, he could not imagine how he would kneel without splitting the trousers. What would the Denham-Cookes say if this crisis arose?

I felt ill. I had a few days ago had a bad attack of influenza, and having got over the worst, we hoped, the doctor suggested I should be buoyed up with brandy. I have never been an ambitious tippler and by midday I was in an inebriated daze.

In this daze I drove over to Frinton, where it seemed the whole of the British Army were lining the street. The tiny church was already full as I tottered into it, to stand mutely whilst they sang that unending 'Voice that breathed o'er Eden', my father on my left, deeply and vigorously bass, and the best man on my right, in a pathetic falsetto. The service started late because the three clergymen had disagreed in the vestry. The local incumbent, the regimental chaplain, and the head chaplain all fighting about which bit of the service the others should take, and apparently all wanting the vital bits for themselves.

I thought I should drop. Never have lilies shaken more twitteringly than they did that day!

In the end it passed off reasonably and there was one agonizing moment when I heard an appalling crack beside me and thought my father's trousers had gone bang; in my agony I let my lilies slip for good. It was really the best man who had been nothing but a nuisance from the first and dropped his prayer book. In the foggy vestry nobody kissed me. I was introduced for the first time to my new brother-in-law Lord Arthur Hill, who had married Mimi, Arthur's half-sister. It was something of a shock to marry a young man of twenty-five and find you have a brother-in-law advanced into the seventies, but that was what happened. I had never seen more black overcoats with astrakhan collars, and I left that church not realizing that none of my new in-laws intended to honour the reception but returned at once to London.

I never saw the archway of swords, or the confetti, or the soldiers. In the car Arthur said, 'I hope you'll never regret this,' but I find all gentlemen say that when you marry them, for the same solicitation was repeated by a naval officer (at that very moment playing Pin Pool in

Hong Kong) nine years later on.

The reception was dreary, and it was regrettable that later the officers of the Queen's hit on the delicious idea of going out on to the greensward and having a game of hockey with their swords, which got them into serious trouble later on with the C.O. who was definitely *not* amused. I drove away in a Daimler car wearing an impressive matron's toque, which I prayed would make me look really old. That illusion vanished in the hall when Richard Aldington's mother said, 'Darling little Ursula doesn't look fifteen, does she?'

I did not kiss Mother goodbye. I couldn't do it. I hope she understood.

I passed out just beyond the level crossing. It was all that brandy! My hat fell off, and Arthur put his boot through it in error, so the matron's toque served no purpose whatsoever. We pushed it out of the window just before we got to Colchester, because it looked so peculiar that we could take it no further with us.

'Dammit, I'll never get married again,' Arthur told me as I fainted, recovered, then fainted again, and he whipped a flask out of his pocket. 'I've emptied it five times myself already, now you have a go!' he suggested.

Believing that gentlemen always knew best, I did have a go, which only made me worse. We stayed that night at Berners Hotel, where all the older men wore armlets with G.R. on them (George Robey had said, 'All those jolly decent chaps who wear my initials on their armbands'), for these were men under Lord Derby's scheme. Early next morning Arthur went off to visit Ma, which was a mistake for they had a shocking row, whilst I went out shopping. Mother had given me two pounds to spend, and I went to Selfridge's and sent it to her in food parcels, which gave me immense joy. When I came back I was being paged, but as I did not recognize the name as being my own I took no notice, which was the reason why I was very late at Lord Lurgan's lunch-party, another blot on my unhappy copybook.

Later that day Arthur and I and the lady's maid went down to Bournemouth which Ma had insisted was the only place for a respectable honeymoon, and as we had only a very brief leave, we returned the next morning and dined that night at a small dinner-party at Prince's Gate. Ma did not attend it, and I rather wished my sister-in-law had kept away, for she was no help to me.

Just when I was breaking down, the kind old butler offered me a pudding and lowered his head close over me. 'Don't pay any attention to any of them,' he whispered.

I have always been eternally grateful to him for his goodness of heart; he was a darling and the best of the lot, as I have said before.

On the return journey to Frinton I broached a subject near my heart. We had this large house of ten bedrooms, half of them empty, and I did not want Mother to continue at The Cedars. I wanted to get her into my own house with me. Arthur looked at me and frowned.

'It could not be for very long,' I said humbly, and then in bald words, the confession I had never made before because it hurt too much: 'She is dying.'

He said: 'Ma's been dying for years, didn't you know? Mummy'll see Ma out.'

'I don't think so.'

He was definite. 'Ma said you'd try to do this, and it's no good. This is our home and our home it is going to stay. I'm not having it any other way.'

I dared not argue.

We drove home on that bitter night, and on entering the hall found all the servants lined up to wish us well, marshalled by the butler. I wished them anything but well. Arthur shook hands all round, and ordered a bottle of port and another of sherry for the kitchen to drink our health, and I went to my room. Even that was no longer my own, for there was the personal maid wanting to know 'which evening gown Madam would require'.

The only consoling note was from Joscelyn. Earlier in the year I had sent him certificates to apply for compassionate leave to come and see Mother. I dared not tell her of this, in case it was refused; now it had been accepted and he was already on his way. He would be back by December.

When I approached Arthur about this, he agreed to our putting Joscelyn up, for he was in a jovial mood, but within the week some idiot in the mess said to him, 'So now you've got all the family hanging round your neck, haven't you?'

That started trouble!

There was no doubt about it, he had a violent temper, and the first time I saw him go white with rage and throw a decanter across the room, I very nearly collapsed. I had never known that people could behave like that, and when he recovered a trifle I said so.

'But darling nincompoop, that's nothing!' said he. 'One of my ancestors strangled his valet in a rage! A grandsire shot a footman. We're nice little fellows when you get to know us!'

He did not understand that a new diamond brooch did not settle a scene of that sort, and felt that I was unreasonable. It all came of that daft country rectory where I had been brought up, and where nobody knew how many blue peas made seven!

The Times had raised its price to a penny-halfpenny. Ruination, said Mother. Other papers became a penny, and this at the time when all the world was thinking that the war would go on for ever, and believing that the only decent thing it had produced was *The Bing Bays are here*, with Vi Loraine and George Robey singing:

If you were the only girl in the world,
And I was the only boy …

Food tickets were on the way. Just at first I was confronted with the agonizing experience of trying to housekeep on six guineas a week and feed five servants who ate like horses, and who would not conform to voluntary rationing. The personal maid was the worst. She turned up her nose at margarine, which we felt should cover one meal a day. 'I'll teach her!' said Arthur. 'Nothing but margarine is to be served in the dining-room.'

So margarine *was* served in the dining-room, which alas only made more butter for the kitchen, and set him gibbering with rage. I said that all my life I had dressed and undressed myself, and could see no reason why I could not continue to do it this way. He felt that Ma would think it was wrong if I did not have the personal maid. Nothing, thought I, could be more unpleasant than *having* her, but I dare not argue.

In spite of the food troubles, at that very time Whiteley's were advertising hams at one and eightpence a pound, Christmas cakes from four shillings to five guineas (inscribed with Allied flags and colours), and an enchanting item which intrigued me called an 'Entente Gateau', a fresh Genoa cake, decorated with Allied flags or representative colours (one and ninepence and three shillings).

There was an unfortunate incident when the glass coffee percolator which had been a wedding present blew up at dinner, bursting like a bomb and nearly drenching the butler. This was the first occasion on which I had heard bad language, for until that hour in my girlish innocence I had believed that 'damn' and 'blast' were the only swear words in existence. I was quickly disillusioned.

Mother was now giving the brave impression that all days were 'good' days. She went to the Radium Institute for treatment; she looked forward to Joscelyn's return on furlough. We did not talk naturally any more, because we couldn't. A barricade rose between us, I had always the curious feeling that in marriage I walked on a quicksand, and she must have known it; the fact that she asked no questions should have warned me of this.

My father never wrote at all. It seemed that he had gone right out of our lives.

Arthur was convinced that red wine would be the right thing for me. The fact that I didn't drink, that I had always hated the taste and the smell of it, and felt miserable if I took it, caused constant controversy. Aristocratic ladies drank, he said, I must become used to it.

Every morning at eleven the butler brought me a glass of port on a salver, and a macaroon. Just at first I drank it, to discover that immediately afterwards I slithered into a giddy confusion which never cleared until after lunch. I reeled. It was a horror lest the butler or the genteel one should find me in this unhappy condition; so as I could not get out of taking the port, I arranged to lie down on the sofa, take it, and stay where I was until such time as escape was possible.

Every eleven o'clock was a menace to me. Worse still, I never got any better. How long it would go on I could not imagine, and shrank from the indignity of being trained to be an aristocratic young lady who delighted in strong drink.

'You'll get used to it; the thing to do is to keep on,' said Arthur calmly.

I never have got used to it to this day.

Joscelyn appeared in Frinton one December midnight, and because he had no wish to knock us up, had a doss-down with a friendly soldier. The soldier was in Arthur's company, so the first social gaffe was committed. At seven o'clock on a remorseless east coast morning Joscelyn arrived at Thalassa, blue in the face, and with chattering teeth which sounded like tom-toms. The butler came to my room where I and the genteel one were arranging myself for the day, and he told me, 'Madam's brother is in the hall.'

I did the unforgivable thing, for I forgot that I was now grand; I rushed out and went sliding down the banister with no frock on, just a princess petticoat, for the exuberance of seeing someone I loved was too much for me. The genteel one looked like the wrath of God, but my brother and I clung together in the hall, and when I came to, I sent a maid out to tell Mother, then tried to get Joscelyn warm. The butler suggested hot rum; it smelt awful, but it did seem to do the trick.

Arthur arrived before Mother, and he seemed gauche so that I immediately sensed something was wrong. I had not realized that officers and private soldiers could not mix under the same roof, and as soon as possible Joscelyn must get into 'civvies'. I, who knew that his suits were only the cheaper kind, and would be hideously creased from storage, hated the idea.

When Mother arrived she sided with Arthur, and took Joscelyn back with her to change. The result was that the first time he went to the shops, he returned with three white feathers presented to him by a patriotic old lady who, although men were conscripted, still thought white feathers were the thing.

'So much for *ich dien*,' said Mother.

The leave was brief. I tried to get him a commission, for that would keep him in England, training with the Inns of Court O.T.C., for some months ahead. By then surely the war would be over? He had endured a difficult journey from Egypt, for the submarines had been insistent. He told Mother of the incident when the best game of chess he had ever played had been ruined by a torpedo only missing the ship by inches. This worried her.

'He won't go back,' I promised her. 'I'll get him a commission somehow. What's the good of marrying well if you can't get it to help you in emergencies?'

I solicited the help of the Brigadier, though he was not as helpful as I had hoped he would be. At this period he was teaching me all the regimental march-pasts of the British Army, and every time he came down he questioned me on the tunes. He knew them, I never did. He taught me how to stand inflexibly at attention, so that to this day I stand like a statue. He then taught me how to salute, and was emphatic about the thumb down the seam of the trousers.

'But my trousers don't have a seam there,' I explained when hopelessly floored.

Arthur thought all this was great fun. He liked me to become militarized. As I was getting on at my lessons I thought the Brigadier would help me, but the bother was that nothing was as easy as it had been.

Life's complications were almost overwhelming, and the greatest of all seemed to be having a corporal staying in the same house as a captain. The climatic conditions were dreadful for Joscelyn coming from Gaza to Christmas on the east coast, and nothing happened about the commission.

He came, he stayed what seemed to be only a couple of weeks, and then had to go back. I left him alone with Mother to say goodbye, and later I went to her, dreading this, for it would be most difficult. She was sitting very still by a dusty fire, and beyond the windows a fog rolled in from the sea; far away was the boom of an exploding mine. She looked at me, her face ashy. 'I shall never see Joscelyn again,' she said.

I could not deny it. I knew it was the truth and it made me quite sick.

Lloyd George was in power, and youth thought that a good thing. We had had enough of silly old codgers going drivelling on and the wretched war getting nowhere. Now we might get somewhere, after all.

I had managed to get rid of the genteel one. She wanted a week-end leave, and as I dared not dismiss her, I wrote, told her not to return and sent her her wages. She wrote a bitter letter explaining to Arthur how poor we had been at Hertford House, and he promptly answered as only a barrister could. The letter stung me, and made me quite sorry for the genteel one, though I admit that she had asked for it.

Food plots were being planned in Hyde Park. The war was now to be fought with renewed force, and Lloyd George was getting at it. Even if Mother disliked him because he was Welsh, I felt that he was doing the right thing.

Russia had wobbled on the edge of defeat for some time, and suddenly we got the news that Rasputin had been murdered. I was horrified by the gruesome details as I read the news at breakfast.

'Oh, I wouldn't fret myself over old Rasputin,' said Arthur airily. 'Of course it's butchery, but this is a butcher's war, and the whole ruddy lot of us are at it.'

'It isn't nice,' I commented.

'Of course it isn't nice. There are lots of other things that aren't nice either, and one of them I want to talk to you about, it's something that has got to be settled. Listen, my angel. I'm going to get busy.'

He told me of the night when the C.O. had sent him to search Hertford House because of the report that Mother and I were spies. He had thought the rumour was dead; it wasn't.

'Oh, not again?' I begged him.

Just after his wedding a captain of the 23rds had said, 'Didn't you marry that girl they thought was a spy?' He had knocked the captain down, only to find that he was senior to himself, and there had been a frightful row. He had told me nothing about it at the time because he thought it would upset me, but he would have gone to chokey or have dropped a pip or something shocking, if the Brigadier had not come into it.

The Brigadier seemed to be the ever-ready help in trouble, and I let that one pass. At the same time I was embarrassed for Arthur now wanted to unearth the whole of a scandal which I wanted to leave buried. He had made enquiries and had found that two of his subalterns had been billeted at a certain house in Walton where the landlady had repeated the story, adding: 'Those Blooms ought never to have been allowed to come to this place. They are responsible for a lot of our trouble.' He now intended to force an issue.

'If you get a feeble enough mouse, it squeaks,' he told me, 'that's what I'm going to do, then I'm coming down with the law. Public apology everywhere, and sweep the path clean.'

'Oh no, Arthur, don't do that.'

'If people throw enough mud it sticks. I'm unsticking it, and be damned to the old lady.'

'But why that old lady? She was really rather nice.'

He said: 'You're too good to live. I've had the misfortune to marry an angel, and her wings are always ruffling me up the wrong way. This is going to be settled, my dear, and for good.'

Both the subs. were to dine with us that night, and I was apprehensive. It was an amiable enough dinner, and before we had gone very far I realized that the wine was flowing a good deal faster than the young men could take it. Arthur never turned a hair with wine, I had found that out early in our marriage, so he was entirely in command of a situation when they were already in deep water. He steered the conversation to that nice old lady where they had been billeted. They told him what she had said as something of a jolly good joke, and how he laughed! Well versed in cross-examination, he led them on and over the coffee with butler and parlourmaid gone, how they floundered into the trap! Then Arthur changed.

'Now,' said he, 'you two will sign statements.'

'I beg your pardon, sir?' said the senior sub.

'I am writing down what you heard the old lady say, and you are signing it.'

They argued. They said she was quite a nice old auntie, rather a fool of course, but she didn't mean a thing, and anyway this would be jolly hard on her. I was stone silent.

'It's a jolly sight harder on my wife,' said Arthur. 'You chaps will sign on the dotted line. It's a command.'

'I'm damned if I see why,' said one.

'If you are talking to me, kindly address me as sir,' Arthur rapped out. 'I presume you two were not lying about all this; if so, then I shall sue you. You may have repeated it to others. Somebody is going to suffer for this, it is you or the old lady. Which is it to be?'

They signed.

From my end of the table (and the person most concerned), I was cold with horror. I felt it was hardly cricket. To get them here to break bread with us, to give them a surfeit of wine which Arthur knew was intoxicating, and then when they were bewildered to make them sign, seemed like hitting a man below the belt. Maybe I was smug. Maybe I was hallmarked 'Rectory', but surely this was too much.

'Oh, damn your eyes, shut up!' said Arthur.

I wasn't used to that form of address; it had never been used to me before, and I hung back a little dazed, not sure of what was happening. Maybe I had deserved it, but I *was* worried.

Next morning Mr. Stanley Nicholson the local solicitor called on Miss Brannon, who immediately denied having said anything. He showed her the paper which the unhappy subalterns had signed, and she burst into tears. She signed a statement admitting her guilt, which to her horror was published in all our papers and most of the London ones, and she had to pay for it. When I heard this I was furious.

'It's mean,' I said. 'Clear my name by all means, but don't make her pay. You can't realize what being hard-up is, and if she does have to pay let me send her the money.'

It was the Brigadier who told me what he thought of me, in plain English. Men! I thought. Men! I shall never understand them.

From that day to this no one has ever accused me of being a German spy.

The whole of England was now waiting for the spring offensive, for the rationing which must come, for explanations, and most of us still felt resentful and angry about everything that had caused this wretched war.

On January the 25th beer was cut off by half, which made Arthur laugh, for he drank only spirits, and thought that was damned funny. A ration system was already on the way, we were told, and most of us wanted it, for buying food at the moment was very difficult and never satisfactory. Yet all the time we kept dealing with the great problems and the tiny matterless ones in a confusion that was most irritating.

Mother was rapidly growing worse, and I was concerned for her, but whenever I mentioned this Arthur turned angry. His mother was at the back of it. She wanted him to cut entirely adrift from the family, and although he did not tell me this, I knew it was what was happening. My father had never even written to me at Christmas, when I think he was disappointed with the three pairs of socks that I sent him, which must have seemed a poor return for the marriage settlement.

But when Christmas came, I had found it impossible to get the money to buy gifts. Mrs. Denham-Cookes had warned Arthur that I should be extravagant, so he refused to give me any personal allowance, but said I had only to ask for money and it should be mine. I asked for money to buy Christmas presents and it was instantly refused. I got frightened.

I don't understand this man, I told myself. All the time extraordinary things were happening. Often at night he would disappear for hours at a time. He had most curious fainting attacks which made me afraid to leave him alone. He was changeable. First gay and lovable with that Irish charm of his, and then suddenly in one of his violent moods, new to me, and alarming.

I did not dare tell Mother, for I did not want her to know that something was worrying me. Once I said to him, 'I think you drink an awful lot,' and he turned and laughed at me.

'The old teetotal rectory!' he said.

We never had been teetotal; there was beer, there was whisky, there was our own sloe gin and very potent it was, but it was no use arguing, and the last thing I wanted was a row.

'Where do you go at night?' I asked him.

He turned angry.

I could not turn to Mother, and my father seemed already to be lost to me. Joscelyn was on the high seas returning to Gaza, and there was no one else. I felt there was more behind this, and the man who ultimately disclosed it was the butler.

I was sitting knitting by the dining-room fire when

after breakfast he came in with a tray to collect depleted decanters from the side. Amongst them was the handsome one which takes a bottle and a quarter, and which a Great Yarmouth landlady had given me as a child.

'That can't be empty! It was only filled last night,' I said.

Possibly I sounded dismayed, even angry, certainly insistent, for he looked at me. 'Yes, madam,' he said, and then as I protested, 'I am a teetotaller, madam,' and he went out of the room.

I saw then those strange facts of which I had been so strangely unaware. In the rectory this condition was unknown to me. The labouring man revealed his condition by his gait and manner, but this was a sickness. It was far more serious than the 'blind' and the thick head; this was not the ordinary or the accepted, for Arthur was a very sick man, and he had no one to help him, save myself. I was unqualified to do much (whatever happened Mother must never know), but something would have to be done.

At eleven he came in, walking across the frosted lawn, his spurs jangling. He looked ill, I thought, too thin, his face too flushed, the skin puffed round his eyes. I asked about the decanter, and instantly he flew into a temper; when that had quietened down, and I had stood my ground, suddenly he told me the truth.

It had always been like this. It had begun as a child, when the shyness and the shame over his hand had worried him; when they had stayed in France and Ma had given him brandy in the water, to make it 'safe for him to drink'. It had become worse when he grew older. He could not go to Eton because he had pneumonia, and when he went to Trinity Hall, Cambridge, that was the first time that he had gone anywhere away alone. His hand had made it difficult for him, and he had had to steel himself against comment. He had hoped I would never discover.

'We've got to get this cured,' I said.

'You don't mean – you can't mean that there is a chance? Och, but I'd give the world for that, I'd do anything, suffer anything; darling, help me?'

'I will, of course.'

'You'll never leave me? That's what scares me.'

'How could I leave the man I married?' I asked, the old rectory training to the fore.

We had got to fight this together, and this was the trouble, because I knew my own inability to help. Besides, now he admitted that something was happening in the orderly room, something about which I could not be told. He had made a silly mistake, something trivial, but the Colonel was making a fuss about it.

That evening Mother returned from deep X-ray treatment, and I went to meet her. She had had a difficult journey down, coinciding with a nasty daylight air-raid on London. She had a bad cold and went straight to bed, and I said I would go back after supper. She looked to have aged considerably, could hardly speak, and I knew felt very ill, but I did not know what to do. Over the dinner-table I suggested that we had her here in Thalassa; instantly Arthur bridled up. He had some reason for violent refusal, perhaps because he was afraid of her malady, perhaps because Ma spurred him on, perhaps no real reason at all.

'We'll go and see her together later,' he said.

We went, for I had something to tell her, something of which I was suddenly shy, and I was embarrassed and wanting to hold back. I was going to have a child in the autumn. Yet when I got to her I could not tell her; Arthur was the one who did it.

Mother looked at me, then she said, 'You go downstairs, Arthur, and let me see after her,' then when he had gone: 'However you feel about it now, this is going to be the best thing that has ever happened to us. You're happy with him, aren't you?' Then, perhaps because she guessed something, 'No, don't tell me.'

'I'm happy,' I said.

The next day she was not so well. The cold was worse and the effect of the deep X-rays so bad that the doctor arranged for her to be moved into a home where she could be nursed. He thought the journey, though only half a mile, would be a trial, but it would be better for her in the long run. She drove there that afternoon and I could not go with her.

Arthur had come in to lunch in trouble. He looked dreadfully ill, and could not speak until he had had a couple of drinks, then he told me: 'I've got to go to London. I'm in a hell of a trouble.'

'What's happened? Not the Colonel again?'

'Och, the silly old what-not!' He poured out another drink. 'If this goes wrong I might lose a pip.'

'But you *couldn't* lose a pip?'

'Damn it, I could! I've got to get the 'fluence in on it. I'm going to London on Monday.'

'Look here, Mummy is ill; she has had to go into a nursing home.'

'I can't help that, I shall want you with me. You'll have to come.'

'But Mummy …'

For the first time I saw him look changed. Different, and rather frightening. 'I'll make you come,' he said.

I went to see the doctor about Mother, but he did not seem unduly perturbed. I sat with her most of the day, she seemed vague, rather frail, and she slept a lot. I was deeply worried about her. On the Sunday her voice had become far away, and although I begged Arthur to let me stay with her, he refused. I suppose he was afraid for himself. I did not know the circumstances which were surrounding him, and when I rang up the doctor he let me down lightly. I did not realize that he did it because I had the baby coming, meaning it well, but he should never have done it.

I kissed her good night and left her at nine with the night nurse. They woke me before it was daylight. She was dead.

CHAPTER 12

We went to London that day just the same, I in a daze. We had to change at Colchester, and I sat on a seat in a biting east wind, not knowing what was going on around me. In London I prayed for an air-raid. Arthur left me at the hotel whilst he went to see his ma, and he was gone three hours. I never knew when he returned for I had passed out. When I came to, the hotel porter was still arguing with him and he was making a scene. Unhappily there was no air-raid.

Twenty-four hours later we returned to Frinton, he feeling better because Ma had promised to help him, and she had the 'fluence. He was almost gay about it. The night after my mother's funeral, he walked into the dining-room and held out his tunic to me.

'Unpick the third pip,' he said, 'it's no good going about looking silly. This is the unfairest thing that has ever happened in the British Army, but there you are.'

'How *could* they do it?'

'God only knows!' He walked to the sideboard and gulped down a tumbler of something whilst I started on the pips. I was desperately sorry for him, and this would make it so much more difficult to help him. He oughtn't to be in the Army; if I could only get him out of it, then maybe he could go into a home, get treatment, get something, but our hands were so tied.

'You'll help me?' he asked. 'You know I've always got the feeling you'll run away. Ma said you would. Don't do it. I'd be scared of what I'd do if you did, my sweet.' And then: 'I'll confess something. That's why I sleep with the Colt beside me. Don't run away whatever you do.'

The curious thing was that I wasn't frightened, I took his hands. 'You don't realize that I could not run away. This is sickness and I promised to stay. I shall stay, you know.'

He stuck to that Colt all the same.

He was so deeply unhappy, so torn two ways by his mother, by life, and in a way by his deep affection for me. At this particular time I was not fitted to help because the shock of Mother's death had gone deep, and there was the baby coming, too. Besides, I did not know what the answer was.

Next morning Arthur was posted to Holland Gat.

Holland Gat was an encampment on the most dangerous part of the coast. The men who lived in the huts there were known as the 'Hold-on-or-die boys', and that about assessed what it was. With the March of 1917, the general fear of invasion along this stretch of coast was starting all over again.

Arthur went off to the camp, which meant I was left with just the servants in Thalassa, but thank goodness without the genteel one. I was suffering from shock, I felt very ill, and I shrank from other people. First of all they would soon guess that I was going to have a baby, and secondly they must know about the lost pip. That stung me badly. I did consult a doctor about Arthur, vaguely groping for help, and he told me that he thought Arthur was in a bad way. Ultimately, he believed, his brain would go.

You would have thought that doctors could be more discreet, mercifully I did not believe a word he said, and came home in a rage. That was when Ma had got herself busy and had done something about the emergency, and the Denham-Cookes' solicitor arrived. He was the tall aristocratic creature with the yellow drooping moustache and the astrakhan coat collar who had added little to my wedding. He came down on a day when the meat was a shocker, and there were no potatoes. It was the worst lunch I have ever served anyone, and not my fault, though I dare say it looked like it.

We drove out to the camp in a seedy old landau. The best horses were at the front, and we should never have got this dilapidated article save that she had the megrims. However, Mr. Levett did not know that she was liable to fall down at any moment. We were set down at a gate with Holland House across the road, and had to walk the cliff path to the Gat. Sleet was falling. Mr. Levett was Edwardian and although he had the manner of an earl, he could not entirely hide a certain apprehension.

Nearing the camp the inevitable bother began. Something must have been sighted, for the Navy came from Harwich way, as ever travelling so much faster than a landlubber thinks to be possible. Soldiers dashed out of huts, some yelling to us 'Get out', others 'Go home', or 'Come on quick'. It was tricky to know what to do. He went on and into the hut airily alluded to as 'the Mess' (quite the most apt description of it!). I knew that the solicitor hated being there with a pregnant woman, but what could we do?

When Arthur came he told us this had been a false alarm and he and Mr. Levett went off to the far corner and talked in whispers so that I shouldn't hear. In the end they came to a conclusion but I wasn't told what it was. Then we walked back to the waiting cab, with the old horse still standing in the Army attitude. The path seemed to have become stickier, and Mr. Levett was wearing patent shoes which did not take kindly to it. I kept wondering what he was thinking, but he said nothing. In the cab I asked, 'Is this going to be all right?'

He looked at me with pained reserve. 'It is not possible to form any opinion until I am told the argument of the other side,' he informed me.

Left alone at Thalassa I felt desperately unhappy. The death of my mother had been a severe shock, for although I had realized that it was near, I had never thought it could be so soon. My father re-married within the month, Joscelyn was far away, and I was now painfully aware of Arthur's trouble, and wanting to save him. I consulted the local doctor, who was not very friendly. I got in touch with the Army one, who was a charming young man, but unfortunately he spoke the truth. This was the worst type of case. The fact that Arthur was in the Service made it difficult to do much for him; there were treatments, he launched himself into a list of such, which were double Dutch to me.

I said: 'I oughtn't to be having this baby really. It seems so dreadfully unfair.'

He agreed but avoided my eyes.

In the end he went back to his wife with a large bunch of daffodils, and I was left to have that good cry which did not appear to be a help any more. It almost seemed that if the Huns landed (and at this moment there was every fear) and we were all annihilated, that could be the answer. At Holland Gat the orders were *No Retreat*. Evacuation papers were flittering about again. My own private troubles seemed very small against the troubles of England at this particular hour.

I read magazines over the fire, they had always fascinated me, and I wrote to the help page in *Home Notes.* Here is the answer which I received.

HOME NOTES
18, Henrietta Street,
London, W.C.2

A. Pearson.

My dear Reader,

Thank you for your letter. I am so very sorry for you in your anxiety about your husband, and sympathize deeply with you in what you must suffer. The cure I referred to in my article was …

I do hope very much that you may be able to induce your husband to undergo the treatment, and if so will you be kind enough to let me know the result? It is so much more satisfactory to me to know if my help has really helped. Please write again if I can do anything more for you, and I very gladly will.

Always your friend,

ISOBEL

If, as I read the letter for the first time, anybody had told me that ten years later I should myself be in Isobel's post – and hold it for seven years – I should never have believed them.

The war itself was going badly. I got scared to open the newspapers, and all the time we kept hearing of young men from the regiment who had landed only a few hours in France, to die. The enemy seemed to be strong as ever, and I think all of us were forced for the first time to admit the wretched truth, that we *could* lose the war.

In the kitchen we were trying to make maize bread,

the most revolting cakes with potatoes and grated beans, and because chocolate had now become desperately short, some home-made stuff with cocoa-butter. Mrs. Fanthorpe made me a lot of this, for she knew I loved chocolate and could not get it, and thought that as I had a baby coming, I had better be a bit spoilt. I never dared admit that I could not eat it. I tried giving it to strange children on the greensward, but they had an unpleasant habit of tasting it, then throwing it down and looking evil at me. I threw it down the cliffs, I jammed it into gorse bushes, and still she went on making it!

Cocoa-butter chocolate was one of the nastiest things this wretched war had ever invented for us!

However, Mr. Levett had managed to get into action. It took him his time, he wasn't the sort whom one could bustle, but one afternoon in May Arthur's batman came over on a bicycle to tell me that Arthur was transferred to the Durham Light Infantry.

'The Captain's going to Falmouth, madam,' he said with the loyal adherence of his men who adored him and still would call him 'the Captain'. 'Posted for next week, he is. A bit of all right, I'll say, madam!'

A bit of all right it was!

In a seventh heaven we prepared to flit. Arthur was to go down four days ahead and get a furnished house for us. I'd follow with a couple of maids. He gave me a cheque for fifty pounds to clear up everything, and his mother sent Jim, his old nurse, to 'keep an eye on me'. Jim was a typical upper servant, grand, dignified, and prepared to go back to Prince's Gate to Mrs. Denham-Cookes with I-have-a-tale-to-tell-oh! She didn't like my servants, she didn't like me, and the row we all had over her early morning tea in bed was a short story in itself.

The day before I was to start for Falmouth, a sour-looking man appeared from the local wine shop and asked to see me. I went to speak to him and he presented me with a bill for over eighty pounds, and a nasty note saying that if I did not pay it immediately a writ would be issued.

It seemed to me to be a fantastic sum. Never could I believe that we had spent so much. I offered the man the sapphire and diamond bracelet and my engagement ring, but he took great exception to my honesty of purpose and started to bluster. Never had anything like this happened to me before. I telephoned to Stanley Nicholson to come over from Walton, and asked the man to wait. He said he wouldn't wait very long, money was what he wanted, and money was what he was going to get. I explained that I did not see how, but apparently he did, and he was right. Mr. Nicholson came over on his motor-bike, and said that the bill must be paid and he would cope. He had a word with the sour-looking young man and got rid of him. I pointed out that when I had paid everybody's railway tickets, the milk and baker's bills, and the little extras that seemed to be popping up at every point, I should have about thirty shillings left. He was reassuring. He would pay the bill and Arthur could pay him back.

'He won't be pleased,' I said.

Very kindly he said: 'You leave me to deal with him and don't worry. It'll be all right.'

The maids left at seven next morning. At nine I and Jim, and Juliet the pug dog Mother had left me, started off on an unbelievable journey. Jim saw me off at Paddington at one, and I could get no lunch. The train was due in at Falmouth at eleven-ten at night! I don't think Jim was sorry to part with me, I certainly had no regrets about getting rid of her, for she had done nothing but complain and I could not think why she had ever been thrust upon me. The journey was monotonous and dull. When we got to Plymouth I saw the Navy in great display and found that fascinating. (The next time I was to come there was to meet the Sub-Lieutenant who at that moment was serving in Hong Kong, and who was then unknown to me.)

I thought Devonshire was lovely, and admired the red earth and the pastureland, but we seemed to be going on for ever. Darkness came. Here there seemed to be no blackout for to my amazement blinds were not drawn and lights twinkled gaily like stars. When I got to Falmouth station I was very, very tired.

Arthur met me and we drove to the little old-fashioned terrace above the park in which he had taken a house. En route I confessed about this awful bill that Stanley Nicholson had paid.

'Oh my God!' said Arthur.

'Has it – has it ruined us?' I stammered greatly concerned.

He was furious that anyone had had the impertinence to pay it. Of course we didn't owe it! How could we have drunk that much? 'How indeed?' I murmured tactlessly. He flew into one of those ungovernable rages which were so agonizing, and then collapsed in the front garden of the house, so that I had to drag him inside and only pray that the servants had gone to bed and would never know.

He wept when we went to bed, and I lay there after he fell asleep, with the blinds drawn and the lovely flower-scented air coming in through the window, and lights still burning on the other side of the park. It seemed a quite unreal world. All the time there was the loaded Colt by Arthur's side.

Falmouth was fascinating.

It was an immense relief to be away from the gruelling pressure of the constant war on the east coast, and also from men and women who knew that my husband had lost a pip. Falmouth was a city of flowers, of calm, an oasis where nobody bothered about blackouts and treated them as being so much nonsense. The war news had improved from the moment we got down to Cornwall; food was more liberal there, and barring the immense trouble Mrs. Fanthorpe the cook had with the Cornish oven, life was considerably easier.

I sat and sewed in the park, where a band played in the afternoons. I went down to the beach in the bay, and admired a far more turquoise sea than the one at Frinton. Nobody was washed up. The wreck of a torpedoed ship in the bay, its masts rusting out of the water, was the only indication that there was a war on at all. The unreal atmosphere did not endure for long for the absence of the blackout was changed abruptly on the night of a dance in the mess. The lights were streaming out into flowery gardens, the windows wide open and the regimental band playing 'Let the great big world keep turning', when the great big world started turning in a different way! A second lieutenant, white as a sheet, shot into the room and said something to the Colonel, who immediately clung on to his chair for support. A submarine had been sighted in the bay, they thought it was an enemy one! Women fainted. People rushed to the blinds which refused to be drawn, being quite unused to the effort now made on them. No shot was fired, but a glorious panic began; I have never seen people so frightened. At the end of an hour the dance broke up, one of the senior officers being left on the mess sofa in a dead faint. This amused Arthur considerably; he thought it the funniest thing he had seen in years.

Falmouth resigned itself to the blackout. They talked of the submarine for days, and reckoned they had been in dire danger. Suddenly we started to be more careful about food, for wheat was now the worry, and the King's proclamation exhorting his subjects to food economy had been read from the steps of the Royal Exchange by the Common Crier of the City. This impressed Falmouth.

The little hand-carts with gleaming fresh mackerel straight from the sea did a terrific business. We dined out most nights at the Green Bank Hotel, most romantically situated at the harbour head, hanging over the water so that you could imagine you were at sea, with no danger of being sick.

The news came that the D.L.I. would soon be drafted overseas; Arthur was rapidly worsening. He was collapsing in comas and was constantly being brought back from duty in a state of semi-consciousness. The civilian doctor did not like him, and was annoyed with me because I did not intend to have the baby in Falmouth. He told me that unless I could do something about getting Arthur into what was then known as a 'cushy job', he would be sent overseas to some outpost of empire to relieve an AI man, and would die there.

This did not cheer me. We got leave and went up to London to get the 'fluence to work. It was at that time a ten-hour trip, as the trains being considerably reduced stopped at every station. The previous day, July the seventh, there had been a dreadful daylight air-raid, killing 57 and injuring 197, which fraught the visit to London with doubt. This very week hot-weather kit was being issued to the troops, and already I had seen too many columns march away, with weeping wives and those courageously dry-eyed mothers waving them goodbye. This was a race with time.

We went to Prince's Gate. I could not be admitted. The difficulty was that I was pregnant and my mother-in-law said that it would be improper for the butler to see me. I had to sit outside in the taxi where an ancient maidservant brought me milk and cake, whilst Arthur and Mrs. Denham-Cookes had one of their more tempestuous rows within. They were the most extraordinary family, having quarrels the like of which I hope never to see again (once I saw Arthur rush up the stairs flourishing a loaded Colt ready to shoot his mother), but they came out of them on a fairly even keel in the long run.

Arthur was to get a job in the Ministry of Pensions. It was, he said airily, merely the job of sitting by a wastepaper basket, as far as he could make out, and if he went into a coma, he would just flop into the wastepaper basket, so that would worry no one. We drove to Berners Hotel, where a *contretemps* immediately ensued. It was difficult to get spirits these days and if Arthur did not get sufficient, the comas and the shaking began. I went out into Oxford Street, only hoping that no one would notice how very pregnant I was (in those days it was considered to be rude), and I stood in a queue outside a bar where I managed to get some brandy. The price was appalling, three pounds if I remember rightly, but I brought it back in triumph.

We were two young people in a blind alley. He had no right to take more yet could not live without it. Maybe the baby would put it all right. I wonder how many girls have thought that?

There was another unpleasant scene at Prince's Gate before we returned to Falmouth,when he and Rowland got wrong whilst I was sitting outside in the taxi. The ever-ready Colt was whisked out, and had it not been for the intervention of that much-harassed butler, I think somebody would have been shot that time. How the butler survived life there I have never been able to understand, for although I only sat on the fringe of it, in the car innocently drinking milk and eating buns, I saw enough to put me off.

We started back again on the ten-hour journey to Falmouth and the anxiety was only lest the new posting would not come in time. Four days before the D.L.I.'s departure for an unknown destination, Arthur came rushing back from camp on a borrowed bicycle. He was radiant. He was a new man and the 'nice little fellow when you got to know him'. The 'cushy job' had come through!

We had a final glorious dinner at the Green Bank Hotel, when he gave five pounds each to three waiters and the head *maître d'hôtel* and left them almost dumb with amazement. We then went to an upstairs room for a little music, had an exciting party which grew more exciting as the night progressed, and finally a very red-faced admiral, who was doing a *pas seul* sword dance with a naval and an infantry sword crossed, had a wastepaper basket popped on to his head and banged down so that he got stuck in it! I had been sitting in a far window-seat which looked out to sea, trying to hide the fact that I was in the so-called interesting condition, and crying quietly to myself.

I felt alone. I never have been much good at drunken parties, and in the end we had to flee the place, five officers and myself, and Arthur gave the night porter a ten-pound note as a parting gift.

I imagine that the Green Bank were very sorry to say goodbye to us!

There was another ten-hour journey back to Berners Hotel. The first thing to do was to arrange with a specialist for the baby, and I went to that most charming man, Jock Hedley. We went down to some friends of Arthur's in Dulwich who helped us take a furnished house there, 82, South Croxted Road, where the baby would be born in October. It looked quite pleasantly secure. The maids came up from Falmouth at once and we settled in.

My great difficulty was the fact that I had no money, for even now Arthur would never allow me to have any in case I ran away from him on it. It was an obsession with him. He would pay for anything I wished, but I could not have the money to pay myself. I wanted things for the baby, I wanted sets of new undies which would cope with my changing figure, and how that figure was changing!

'If you want more underclothing, let me come with you and buy what you want, I'll pay,' he said.

We went to a famous shop and I bought some lingerie, he sitting by on the small chair set for such a purpose, and going scarlet. I could not think what was the matter. When we came out he was torn between laughing and fury, for the girl who had served me had been the one he had known as a waitress at Cambridge and who had tried a breach of promise on him!

'Be ye sure your sins will find you out,' said he brightly.

'Why not let me buy my own undies in future?'

But, oh no! Nothing of the sort. In the end I had to deceive him. He was extraordinarily stupid about cashing cheques, and was always getting stuck for ready money, and I had managed to get five pounds put by. I would cash him a cheque for five pounds if he gave me ten shillings for doing it. Fair enough, said he, and did. On these miserable ten shillings, I bought the baby's clothes, and a cot I trimmed myself (it cost seventeen-and-six at the grocer's of all places!), and so became equipped for the great moment. He went home to see Ma every few days, usually the most unfortunate visits ending in one of their crashing rows, but I was mercifully off the map for the moment. I was now wholly in purdah.

When we had taken this house neither of us had realized that the Royal Navy were stationed in the Crystal Palace at the top of the hill. When I heard they were there I thought it very silly of them. The Crystal

Palace seemed to my simple mind to be no place for those who go down to the sea in ships. Three nights after we had moved in, delighting in the safety of this most excellent position, I discovered what the Royal Navy were actually doing, for an air-raid started.

'Specials' appeared from everywhere on their feet or on their bicycles, and there were the long piercing blasts on police whistles. From just over our heads the most shattering noise began. It was like an extremely bad thunderstorm, and although they might be camping there under the pseudonym of the Silent Service, most certainly they were far from silent that night when they went into action.

'This is awful,' said I.

'Exciting,' said Arthur. 'Jolly good fun. Och! Let's go out and see what it's all about.'

We took a couple of kitchen chairs into the garden where we thought we should get a better view. A plane was hit. We saw it come down, and cheered valiantly, not realizing that it was one of our own. Whilst all this was going on little pieces of metal began to rattle through the air, dropping like hail about us. It was shrapnel, my first introduction to it. We should have gone on sitting there but fortunately Arthur got a stinger on the hand, and at the same moment there was a devastating crash just across the road where a greenhouse had been hit. We went indoors.

I believed that we had rounded a difficult corner, in that the Ministry job would last till the war ended, and Arthur would be safe there. He visited his mother, I always being left outside; each time they had shocking rows, and when it was not Ma it was his sister, and the Colt always came out. One day, I was convinced, there would be some frightful accident.

The war was drifting along with no sign of peace in sight. Arthur was having constant comas, I still believing that they were some strange kind of faint, and terrified to let him out of my sight for a moment. It would be worse when the monthly nurse joined up with the family and things had to be explained, or covered in some way or other. But better when the baby came. Surely the baby would put everything right?

CHAPTER 13

The nurse arrived on the first of October from Brighton where she lived. There she had not had to face war conditions and I sensed the fact that she was very nervous. The first night, during dinner, trouble began at Herne Hill and the Crystal Palace guns opened fire. Because of her distress we did not go to bed until two in the morning, until the Boy Scouts' bugles came by. It had not been a fortunate evening, and I made it worse by having during the morning laid my hands on what I had thought was a regular triumph, a hare for jugging. During the meal someone discovered that the hare was a cat (they were selling chopped up cats like this) and I, fostering rectorial faith in the man who said it *was* a hare, had been deceived.

I tried to explain to the nurse that Arthur was ill, but she did not believe me. We felt her criticism, we shrank from her, a little lost, holding hands under the rug in the car with her sitting on the seat facing us. Oh well, anyway it isn't for ever, I kept telling myself, but the baby did not appear.

The Jerries seemed to be taking an evil delight in the nurse being with us, for there were bombs on the Serpentine and all manner of dead fish floating about, bombs on Victoria station (and she had arrived there, a discrepancy we tried to smooth over for her), and the Royal Academy was damaged.

The accepted date for the arrival of the baby came and went. October was moving over to its end, and I had to admit that Arthur's condition was getting quite frightful. Four days a week he was sent back in a coma. One afternoon he came home saying he had been given a week's leave and then must go into King's College Hospital for treatment. The week was obviously with the idea of my being obliging and having the baby and at least getting that over.

'What can I do?' I asked the cook.

She suggested skipping, and oh, how I skipped! I am now convinced that no one in this world can skip an unwilling baby into this world. The tweeny suggested jumping off the chest of drawers; she had a friend who wasn't able to get her baby into being, and it had worked wonders for her. I did not fancy the idea.

Arthur was worried to death, and had taken against the nurse. He thought it might be the end of all our worries if he shot her!

The week passed and there was no baby. On the Monday I drove with Arthur to King's College Hospital, he shivering with apprehension, hating leaving me as things were, I hating his going. I drove home with the nurse, calm, unmoved, and quite oblivious of what was going on, for anyway tonight she would not be shot, which might be something!

At eight that evening the hospital rang me up, impersonal and indifferent, and enquiring if I was the next-of-kin. That struck cold horror to my heart, and I clung to the sideboard, only praying that he had not died.

Arthur had had an attack, said they, would I come in the morning? I wanted to go right away, but they said no, he was sleeping now, tomorrow would be good enough.

There was no air-raid that night, which was a relief, for the nurse got so bothered about them, and next morning she and I drove to hospital. Arthur seemed to be very ill, shaking terribly and hardly knowing us. But the young doctor was kindness itself; he asked me questions and told me not to be too worried, for they could get him right. Later he would be sent to convalesce at Craiglockhart, a hospital for officers with nervous diseases, in Scotland.

It was something of a shock to see that Arthur had changed so much in those few hours, but I had confidence in the doctor, who was most kind. There *had* to be a daylight raid as we drove home, for it seemed that there was no end to this wretched war; it went on worrying everyone, with not a sign of peace coming even yet.

It was November. The gutters were full of wet dank leaves, and men were mending the road outside the house, which meant that I could not go out until after dark, because in 1917 it would be too humiliating if anyone discovered where babies came from. One afternoon the old butler came down with some clothes from Prince's Gate for Arthur, and one of the maids put him in the drawing-room. I talked to him through the door, explaining that I daren't come in. Very gently he told me that he had three children of his own, it didn't worry him, after which we sat down together and talked. I could not imagine what my mother-in-law would have thought if she ever knew of it, but on that particularly dank November afternoon it seemed one of the nicest things that had ever happened.

Within a few days Arthur was better, and permitted to be fetched out to tea, on condition that tea was all it meant. Joscelyn wrote from Egypt that as far as he could see the war would go on for ever. Still the baby did not come.

The gynaecologist finally decided to operate in the house, and when Arthur drove over to tea I had to break this to him. We rang the hospital together and said that the gynaecologist meant to get things going, and could Arthur spend tomorrow with me, when the baby actually *would* be born (we hoped!)? It took quite a lot of work reconciling Arthur to tomorrow; we had now been six weeks expecting a baby who appeared to be only interested in a stay-in strike.

When I had dispatched Arthur back to the hospital, depressed at what might happen before we met again, the nurse suggested that I should come with her to the cobbler's to fetch some shoes she had had soled. It was a wretchedly dreary evening. Nurse went into the cobbler's, and I stood in the shadows outside, terrified that anyone would see me. There was a public-house there and some of the sailors were singing cheerfully inside. One of them reeled out, was sick in the gutter, then saw me, tottered for a moment, wiped his mouth with the back of his hand and lurched back into the pub. I had the most dreadful butterflies in the tummy, almost a pain, and at that moment I would have given quite a lot of money to be back at home in the rectory, and away from the unhappy condition which I had once thought was marrying into high life.

Nurse and I went home and at ten that night there was the inevitable warning and the Crystal Palace guns started with their familiar gusto. Nurse wanted to stay downstairs; she had a dauntless faith in putting her back against the main wall of the house, which she vowed was completely safe, so I left her at it.

I went to bed and that night I knew that I longed more desperately for my mother than I had done for weeks, for there were times when this passionate desire for her completely distraught me. The sound of bombing came closer, the guns were most vigorous, and half an hour later I realized that something was really wrong with me. I went to tap on Nurse's door, very meekly. There was no reply. Below in the hall a light burnt, and peering over the banister I saw her standing there, still with her back to the wall. It seemed a shame to disturb her but my need was becoming great.

I called: 'I'm so sorry to be a bother, but I think something must be happening. It can't all be my supper.'

It was the baby.

Jock Hedley came immediately. Poor Nurse was in agony, for this was a really nasty raid and it was all taking place on our side of London. In the bedroom the three of us stared at one another. The baby had apparently been coming most of the day, and I had mistaken it for butterflies-in-the-tummy over the operation. I was only worried now lest we could not get the baby born before Arthur arrived at ten next morning, Nurse's worry that we should be hit, and Jock Hedley's agitation a very different anxiety. He had tried to sit down on the chair where the Colt lay. 'Of course it isn't loaded,' he said.

That was when I let out a shriek. 'Don't touch it. It *is* loaded. For goodness' sake don't touch it.'

The raid ended about two o'clock, and the silence seemed strange after all that fuss! They had given me something which made me dizzy and queer; suddenly there seemed to be three doctors in the room instead of one, and the sterilizers made a predominant sound. Jock Hedley was speaking to me.

'If there was no baby would you be dreadfully disappointed? It's being just a little bit naughty! Will you let me do what I want, for I have nobody else to ask, so I've got to ask you? I'll promise to do my best.'

'Whatever you want,' I told him, then slipped back into a deep sleep. At five minutes to ten that morning, just as Arthur arrived, Jock Hedley kept his word and brought the eleven and a half pound baby into the world, a boy.

He wept real tears; he had red hair; he was exactly like my own father, something that I had never expected; and all his finger-nails were very long and had to be cut.

Jock Hedley went downstairs where he found Arthur waiting in the dining-room, and he said: 'Have you seen your son? He's *enormous*.'

Arthur said nothing. He passed out in quite the worst fainting fit of his life, and later when Jock Hedley came up to see me, he admitted that he would much rather have me than my husband as a patient.

Coming to, Arthur gave five pounds to each of the servants, then went off to the West End, buying gold charms for the nurse who collected them, and a bowler hat for the baby, which he thought would be 'jolly useful later on'. I got nothing. There was no comment from Prince's Gate. Mrs. Denham-Cookes had been so sure that I should have a girl, and now that we had got the boy Arthur most wanted, she was indignant.

'We ought to call him Passchendaele,' said Arthur when next day the papers told us Passchendaele had been captured.

'We certainly shall not!' I replied, and he was called Philip. It happened to be my mother's favourite name for a boy, and as I could not call him after her, this was the next best thing.

Arthur and Nurse quarrelled. Disliking his disturbing me she would lock me in my bedroom when she took the baby out, so he could not come in. He would then conduct a blasphemous conversation (about her) through the door which terrified me lest some of the servants would hear and be shocked.

Ten days later Arthur left King's College Hospital, to go to Craiglockhart where he would go before a board and might be invalided from the Army, which I prayed would be true.

Mother had left me her furniture which was now in store at Frinton where I hoped eventually to return, for I felt that it would be such a delightful place in which to bring up a little child. One day perhaps the war would end. One day the bewildering maelstrom in which I was living would change, and then things would be more serene.

Nurse went off to another case, and I was left with abscesses and the plain fact that having a baby was not something from which one recovered in five minutes. My mother-in-law did not telephone or write, but then the poor thing had much to endure for accruing taxation was worrying her stiff. Arthur went before his board, was invalided out with a small pension, and would be coming back to me quite soon, then we should be starting the ordinary civilian life together. Yet when he walked into the house in civvies (I had never seen him in them before) I hardly recognized him. His skin was clearer, his eyes calmer, the cure had worked, for he actually asked for a glass of milk. Yet when we walked out together and a man outside a public-house told him that he ought to be in khaki, instead of letting other poor chaps fight for him, a brawl ensued.

'It's my temper,' he confessed. 'All my family have this Irish temper, though it doesn't mean a thing at all, at all. I hit out. Never mind, it takes all sorts to make a world, and I'm a nice little fellow when you get to know me!'

On Christmas Eve I received a letter Joscelyn wrote to me.

Gaza.
December the 1st, 1917

Dear Ursula,

I'm glad the baby is a boy, but I shouldn't call him Philip. I was five pounds when I arrived, whatever made him do that? The Gyppos say that the war will be over this year. There are constant riots, sandbags and such. I went out on a horse to help a nurse in a wagon who was trying to get through the mob, and they were pretty nasty. I killed the first man I have ever killed and I wasn't sorry, for he was trying to get me and I saw him just in time. He got down into the dust and aimed with a gun, and I split his skull in two with the butt end of my rifle.

The sand makes my eczema bad. Do send me some more thirst quenchers from Selfridge's, and never again send jelly that you have made for me, because the heat melts it and it mucks up everything else in the parcel. You are such an idiot.

Love from JOS.

The queues were lengthening, and all the time the food was becoming much more difficult, whilst all of us were wondering when Lord Rhondda was going to introduce meat rationing which might solve the problem. Although prices were going up, clothes seemed to stay surprisingly cheap, and Harrods were advertising an 'approved outfit' for ladies who were working on the land. The outfit had a Norfolk jacket reaching to just below the hips with two large pockets, shirt blouse, and knickers, all in khaki drabette, guaranteed strong and durable, at twenty-eight and nine.

On Christmas Eve Arthur and I dined at the R.A.C. which managed to produce a quite merry atmosphere.

We were joined by my grandmother-in-law, the dowager Lady Lurgan, who sat down at the table in the gayest mood and was the very antithesis of her daughter. Before long it occurred to me that there was something a little peculiar about Grandmamma. Her voice was high-pitched and extremely loud, and she started to tell us stories which were definitely unsuitable, not to say unexpected, from her. We could only surmise that she had no idea what the words meant.

After a while it seemed to upset the people round us, and Arthur persuaded her to go out with him, then he took her home in the car and handed her over to her personal maid, who was not in the least surprised. 'It's just that her ladyship's been keeping Christmas,' said the maid, and perhaps that was exactly what it was.

The baby was baptized on Boxing Day at Emmanuel Church, almost opposite the house, and not one of his father's family came to the christening, for a titanic row had boiled up and nobody was on speaking terms. Arthur, just returned cured from Craiglockhart, had taken considerable exception to my mother-in-law's method of address when she wrote to him. She had the Victorian habit of abbreviating words, and always began her letters 'My Dt. Artie' (she always called him Artie). He did not want to be a D.T. Artie, and said so. There had been another of those unpleasant scenes, with the butler holding Arthur back, and him brandishing the Colt, scenes to which I was becoming strangely reconciled, and after that nobody spoke.

As the year died we understood that an announcement would soon be made about rationing, and early in February it would be introduced. I had now taken a small house down at Frinton, most unfortunately called Poona, and with the wretched word carved into the stone so that nothing in the world could set us free from it, but to Poona would we go before January died.

Ma had been threatening to stop Arthur's allowance, and he was depressed beyond words about it; also her silence gave us no clue as to what was really happening, so that when she suddenly wrote to him, he was overjoyed.

6, Prince's Gate, S.W.
January 2nd, 1918

My Dt Artie,

I cannot enter into anything in writing, and am not well enough, but I hope that when you are this way you will let me know and come to see me? It is far easier to speak than write. I conclude from gazette that you get Hon. rank of Captain. Army rules are queer these days.

Ever with love,
Your loving

MA

The beginning and the end of the letter provoked much blasphemous comment from my husband, but recovering he rang her up and said he would go to see her. He would ask himself to lunch, always a mistake at Prince's Gate where there was an enormous parade of silver dishes, and only the minutest portions sitting in them.

Several hours later the butler rang me up. Would I please go and fetch my husband home? I drove up in a state of the gravest apprehension, aggravated by the fact that I was immediately admitted, and the moment I saw Arthur I knew what had happened. Someone had given him the key of the tantalus and he was in another coma. I and the chauffeur carried him out to the car between us, the old butler almost in tears, my mother-in-law standing with an ear trumpet poised like a fan on her stomach, in the attitude of the unamused Queen Victoria. From the doorway I looked back at her, it was the last time I was to see her for some years, and although there was a lot I could have said, somehow or other it just didn't come.

We drove home.

We immediately went down to Frinton, lashed by the cold east wind of the turn of the year. The new regiment had wired the front so that it was difficult to walk on the greensward at all, and everywhere conditions had worsened. Although every shop displayed 'Business as usual' placards, business was not at all as usual. My pet butcher had been called up. All the strings I had once pulled seemed suddenly to have snapped. The Sunday joint had gone west and new-laid eggs were four shillings a dozen, which we felt to be a wicked price.

By February two cards were issued to us for rationing, a meat card and a food card. The weekly rates per person were 15 oz. beef or mutton, lamb or pork, 5 oz. bacon, and 4 oz. butter or margarine. The mainstay of life seemed to be sausages. One learnt the hour at which they would be delivered, and lined up at the butcher's with high hope in the heart. When one got the sausages they weren't much, and I cannot imagine what went into them, save all the gristle in the world (Arthur detested it), and occasionally the odd nail that had been swept up with the floor sweepings and popped into the sausage for weight.

Unfortunately wines and spirits were becoming very scarce, and Arthur was again at that stage when whisky was a vital necessity to him. People became well aware of his need; they knew that he was reputed to be 'free with his money', and relied on this, bringing a bottle round at a fancy price. I was for ever finding this happening, for mysterious bottles arrived in his study, sometimes hidden in odd places, and I once found one in the lavatory cistern. 'An original little fellow when you get to know me!' said Arthur.

We were right back where we had begun. It was an

illness, one to which the doctors were in those days severely indifferent. One turned helplessly for help, and got none. I dare not encourage friends to the house lest they should discover too much, or lest he, in his changing moods, should produce the Colt which seemed always to be with him. One day a tragedy would happen, I began to see its shadow ahead of me, and did not know what to do to avert it.

It made matters worse that with the March of 1918 the whole future of the war became so dangerous. On the twenty-first the Germans made the big push and caught us unawares. They came on ahead at speed, and on the twenty-third of the month Paris was once more being shelled, which we had thought we had put behind us for good.

Paris had survived for so long that we had come foolishly to the conclusion that it would keep its present position. Suddenly the enemy was again at its gate, and through that April and the May we expected every day to hear that Paris had fallen. If this happened, there was that vague and secret threat, something we dared not mention, that we might after all lose the war.

On the verandah of Poona, the garden clustering with wallflowers, and the baby in his pram, Arthur said, 'You know, I believe we are going to lose it.'

'What happens to us then?' I asked.

'We bolt to the U.S.A.'

'To get submarined going over! Remember the *Lusitania*.'

'It would be worse to get to the States and all become jolly little Yanks,' he told me.

The morning papers were worrying. The suspense seemed to last for weeks, then suddenly it was announced that the tanks had gone in. This was something new in warfare, the secret of the tanks had been closely guarded, and just at first we could not believe that it was true. They were the great caterpillar vehicles which could go everywhere and conquer everything, even that detestable liquid fire which the Germans so loved using against us.

This meant that the second battle of the Marne had begun. Dare we celebrate on a couple of sausages – if we could get them – and a bar of gritty chocolate? Had we at last rounded the corner? We had.

For some time now I had been taking in dressmaking without Arthur knowing. Something had to be done to save for the education of the baby, for as we were going the money would disappear, and the big income in which my mother-in-law had a life interest would not be ours for some time yet. I never imagined that she would die, although Arthur was for ever putting his shirt on the fact that she was weaker than she used to be, but I never saw it.

I was always sewing so that he saw no new method behind this and asked me no questions. That was satisfactory. Bit by bit I was accumulating a little wad of notes locked away in a dressing-case and in my mind marked Prep., Eton, when the hour comes, and Trinity Hall, Cambridge. But surely by that time something would have happened and we could do better?

At the start of every night Arthur slept heavily, and I would sit up in bed stitching away at orders for war brides, whose number was legion; for ladies requiring *chic* camisoles, and modern young women who sought the Paisley silk pyjama!

We both worked on shifts at the Y.M.C.A. canteen. It was a big hut in the middle of Connaught Avenue, a spacious room with a tin roof which made it very hot in summer and icy in winter. My services had been solicited by Edith Horton, the married daughter of the old lady next door, one of those women who could never think an unkind thought or speak a hard word. I worked on her shift three hours a night and was ready to be called for an 'emergency shift', for troops departed unexpectedly overseas and wanted food before they left. Then the canteen would brim over, and additional staff had to go on duty.

We wore blue cotton overalls with the badge on our pockets and always kept our hats on. Nobody could possibly go on duty without a hat, it would have been considered most improper.

Arthur worked in the post office there and got into constant predicaments over the change. The 'nice little fellow when you got to know him' was at a complete loss when it came to arithmetic, and the soldiers soon rumbled this and made merry on it.

'Look here, sir, two and two's five, isn't it? And you've only given me fourpence, sir. See, sir? It isn't right, sir.'

Privately I reckoned that it cost him ten shillings a night to put his errors right, but it kept him busy, and an interest of this sort was what he needed. He had always been so wildly patriotic that he asked to serve in some small way. The fact that as a soldier his father had done so well and he himself had done so badly, was ever to the front of his mind, but his father had never been menaced with the horror of that deformed hand, which Arthur magnified out of all perspective, and which I have always thought was the destiny which was to shape his life in the long run.

In the Y.M.C.A. we had no labour-saving equipment. The washing-up had to be done in big bowls, with no detergents, and with soaking tea-towels on which we wiped up, and our only amenity was the bread-cutting machine, which, since one of us had taken a finger-tip off in it, none of the girls were allowed to use.

We washed up in the room behind the selling counter

where the two urns mixed their appalling smells of too strong tea and too sour coffee. Along the shelf behind us we had sandwiches of tinned salmon, always the most popular and expensive, the bully beef ones which nobody wanted, the sardine and the potted meat kind. The most expensive drink was *café-au-lait* at twopence-halfpenny, and as a special favour the purchaser was allowed a spoon with it. We had plum cake in slices, and a plain cake that looked like sawdust gummed together, and we also sold cheap sweets, writing-pads, pencils, studs, and buttons, with not much of a sale for any of these.

If you were new on the counter, soldiers would arrive looking pitiful, and offer a penny-halfpenny saying plaintively that they hadn't got any more. Then they would stand looking at the tinned-salmon sandwiches (twopence-halfpenny) and smacking their lips. If this failed, they explained that it did not really matter, for anyway they would be in the trenches by next week. Edith Horton caught me falling for this. She had the angelic temperament which loves every sinner, but she said:

'You mustn't do it, dear, really you mustn't. It will only get us all into trouble, and some of these poor boys are so very naughty. I do wish they wouldn't.'

Then there were the drunks.

One night there was a particularly noisy one, and I was sent along to try to shut him up. We were fussy about this, always sending a married woman instead of one of the girls, which was the rule of the canteen. I failed to stop him and he was using very bad language, so up came Edith Horton.

'You shouldn't do this,' she said to the man. 'What do you suppose your mother would think?'

In no uncertain terms he told us what his mother would think, and what he had always thought of his mother. I should not have expected Edith Horton to understand his language, she was far too nice a woman ever to know anything of this sort, but she accepted it with superb calm, though in the end she had to call up one of the more robust sergeants to throw him out.

Before this started she said to the man: 'It isn't right to say things like that here, or anywhere else. I know you don't really mean it, but all I can do is to have you put out because you go on in this manner. I am so sorry.'

The robust sergeant took it much more sternly than she or I had intended, for he pitched the drunk into a rose bush which we had fondly planted there only the previous week 'to look nice'. It was a Dorothy Perkins which I had brought in a pot to fulfil this obligation, and I was furious.

'Oh, look what he's done!' I gasped. 'My rose bush.'

Edith Horton went to the sergeant. 'How naughty you are!' she said, and when he explained that the man was too drunk to feel a thing: 'Yes, I know, but all the same you shouldn't be rough with him. I don't like it and it's *my* shift. Anyway you've spoilt our rose bush, and if you behave like this you'll have to go as well.'

He grinned, knowing she would never do it. It was her way of running a shift and everybody loved her.

But if the Y.M.C.A. had an amusing side it also had a tragic one. There were those heartbreaking evenings when a draft was off to France, and the casualty lists (whole pages of them in the papers daily) warned us what the chances of survival were.

The men would come into the hut with all their equipment, jingling with Tommy's cookers, tin mugs, and plates, and this would be stacked into the corner amongst bulging bags and stocky-looking rifles. The men had shiny gaunt faces, all of them were trying to pretend that this was just what they wanted, though we knew what sheer hell it must have been to them.

At first those who had laughed too much had deceived me into believing that they did not care. Experience changed my reactions, and now the sound of their laughter was quite sickening. In those hours, it was hard to forget what lay ahead for them.

There were men who gave us last-minute letters to post, 'For my old mum, please, miss,' and there was a new glassiness in their eyes. At the back of every mind there was the memory of those casualty lists, those *awful* casualty lists.

A sergeant would call them to attention outside, and they would be lined up to march to the station. Idiotically we would run out with flowers from the canteen tables, 'for luck', and would take little packets of biscuits to press on them 'to eat in the train'. We spent pounds this way. But whatever we did the white-faced were still white-faced and the hysterical still laughed.

One night I remember a young boy moaning and I went to him; he had been sick. I said: 'It isn't as bad as all that. Quite a lot of them do come back, you know.'

He said: 'What if there was another of these wars? It'd be worse. I'm nineteen, I could live through another ruddy war.'

'There'll never be another,' I promised him, and I thought I spoke the truth. 'What you do today means that my son will never have to fight. There can't be another.' We clung together, then the whistle blew and the young man picked up his gear and marched to his place in the line with all the equipment chattering like the 'rough music' which the village at home had given to neighbours they disliked. One of the sergeants later gave me his name, and on his way across to France the boat was torpedoed.

He was missing before he ever got there.

Still with it all the spy obsession flourished, and

although one would have thought that with the war people would have learnt to think more clearly, they thought more cruelly. I felt particularly horrified over the spy mania, for I had suffered so much, although I had been anything but a spy.

The bitterness never died. That was an era when perhaps we were less aware of conscience, less awake to understanding of humanity as a whole. Other people's sufferings were a matter of some indifference, and I, coming from the rectory, had always been astounded at the Denham-Cookes family who were quite blind to the feelings of others. Save Arthur, who was supremely kind, for I never saw him pass a beggar by; even in his most violent tempers he was never hard to someone who was sick.

Now with the summer waning, and the Huns moving back before our forces, it almost seemed that peace was in sight. We were already making plans. We'd go abroad. We'd visit Ireland, of course, and go to St. Jean de Luz which Arthur loved, to Biarritz and to Nice.

Four years ago we had thought, 'It's bound to be over by Christmas'. Four years on we were now convinced of it. *At last!* It would be the most exciting autumn that we had ever had, and rumour had it that Austria would be the first to collapse. It had come to that.

Whilst we were thinking about it, and almost unable to realize what it would be like to live again without the terrible fear which war nurtured in our hearts, young Gower Robinson now a lieutenant in Hong Kong made a certain entry in his diary. At the time it must have seemed to be quite insignificant, and unimportant to us in England, yet straws show which way the wind blows. Until this hour all our apprehensions and fears and longings had seemed to be for ever across the seas on the fronts, praying that the men would live and return. Now, as the war went further and further from us, it would seem our same apprehensions would be focused back here on England, on ourselves, *praying that we should live*.

Later in this very year the entry of a young lieutenant in his diary would be infinitely significant to us all.

> *Hong Kong. Monday, June the 10th*, 1918
> There is a mysterious epidemic touring the coast ports of China, and it has just arrived here today. There are only 700 men in the dockyard in lieu of 2,400.

That epidemic was called ''flu'.

I read of it in the newspapers later in the summer, on the day that a mine was washed up on Frinton beach, and to cheer myself I went to have a look at it. The casualness with which the people of the First World War treated mines was unbelievable. There it lay on the beach, apparently harmless, round as a globe and quite innocent as far as one could see. A trawler came along from Harwich, and they put off a boatload of sailors who came running up the beach. It amazed me that none of them wore shoes or socks, and that their 'bell bottoms' turned up so beautifully neatly. I was far more interested in the fascinating sailors than I was in any personal danger, for the mine could easily have blown up on us all, but it was a happy matinee entertainment, we felt.

I could not make out what they actually did to it. Whatever they took out of the mine seemed to be extremely difficult to get, and when they had done this they put a chain round the thing, and with deftness got it back into the sea and towed it out to the waiting trawler.

I had taken the baby along in the pram so that he should get an idea of what mines were like; when we got home I told Arthur what fun it had been, and he said that he thought I had been rather silly.

'Mines,' said he, 'are invented with only the one idea, which is to go off.'

I knew that missiles fired which did not go off could be alarming, for the Huns were now dropping a new device on London which we called 'aerial torpedoes'. One had come down in Moorgate and had not exploded, which had made it infinitely terrifying. It had lain in the gutter for an hour and a half, nobody knowing what to do with it, whilst women fainted and strong men disappeared. None of the Second World War promptitude which came along with a label 'Unexploded bomb' with the area cordoned off, ever applied to the original war. People could come and have a look at it if they wished, and if it went off that was just too bad. We had been attacked by, and were incapable of tackling, a modern form of warfare which was still new to us, and it is amazing that we did not pay more dearly for our ignorance.

In the end the Moorgate aerial torpedo went along to Hackney Marshes which was prepared to receive unpleasant gifts of this nature – so they said, I don't know if it was true.

That autumn I went up to London to shop, and London was showing signs of war strain. It was changed. Too many had spent their nights sleeping in cellars and were tired out. The four years were telling. Yet I had a horrid intuition that we still had not faced the worst to come to England. How right I was. In his diary the young naval lieutenant had mentioned it quite casually as people did. It was the epidemic called 'flu.

CHAPTER 14

All pathways by His feet are worn,
His strong heart stirs the ever-beating sea,
His cross of thorns is twined with every thorn,
His cross is every tree.

JOSEPH PLUNKETT
Executed, 1916

Deep depression was now part of poor Arthur's illness, and the tensed atmosphere between himself and his mother did not help. I had no one to whom I could turn, and much as I needed help could not find it. I just sewed on to swell the fund which would ensure the baby going to the right school. Not for the world would I have let anybody know that I was doing this, because I felt it was 'common' of me, and Arthur's family would have said: 'There! What did we tell you?'

I was playing the game of 'let's pretend' with myself, the childish game too many of us play. Something would happen to put things right. I believed in the happy ending.

I hoped for the happy ending. I had a private feeling that life could not be quite as mean as it was apparently trying to be. One day – perhaps tomorrow – everything would come right.

That summer Arthur's college friend Hermon Rogers-Tillstone came down to stay with us. He was a doctor who had had a breakdown, and was now living in Norwich, doing a simple job there which did not strain him too much. It was better for Arthur to have a companion with him, and these days the war seemed to be going further and further away, so that we could relax a little.

'Arthur is very ill, you know,' Hermon told me one day when we were walking on the greensward together.

'I know, but what can we do?'

'Very little, I'm afraid. I thought you ought to know.'

'You don't mean it is anything dangerous?'

'In a way it could be dangerous. His father being over seventy when Arthur was born did not give him stamina. His mother being such an old fool; then that hand. Well, perhaps something will turn up, one never knows.'

I had lived in the hope of that for almost two years. Perhaps it is a joyous thing when one is young enough to believe that somewhere round the next corner there must be happiness.

Hermon and Arthur were great friends, they enjoyed being together, discussing old times, what they intended to do when the war ended, and now in the September it did seem that it must end soon.

Joscelyn wrote:

Gaza.
August the 31st, 1918

Dear Ursula,

All the Gyppos say that the war will be over in a couple of months. As they always know everything this ought to be something. I shall be glad to get back, though in some ways I have half a mind to stop on here with the army. I'm getting used to it. Who would have thought that possible four years ago?

My Tommy's cooker has gone west; is there any chance of getting another one sent out to me? The post caught up with me and there were thirty-two magazines you had sent me. Now the whole camp's reading. Heat awful. *And* how camels smell!

As ever,

JOS.

Somehow now that things were better, and the war horror drifting from us, a lethargy had spread over us. Almost as if we did not care any more.

'Something will happen to stir us out of it,' Hermon said the night before he went back.

It was the very night when after we had gone to bed Arthur thought he heard burglars getting into the house and went down with the Colt. Hermon also, each going a different way round the house and so running into each other in the shrubberies under my window, where the Colt went off. Arthur had mistaken Hermon for a burglar. It seemed a dreadful thought that, after having constantly threatened to shoot somebody all this time, he had now probably shot his best friend! The echo seemed to go on for ever. Perhaps this would be the end. All the same nobody had been hurt, and although the servants were paralysed with fright, we survived.

Arthur was very irritable, he had deep fits of depression, something which the doctors did not help, for from the first they had been horribly unsympathetic. There seemed little we could do, and we just went on always hoping for a miracle.

In the summer Spanish 'flu had been about but it did not come our way. Early in October with the war approaching its end, the front page of *The Times* became alarming. We were accustomed to shocking casualty lists, but the death columns were now enormous and crammed with the names of young people, both men and women, who had died here in England. Their ages seemed always to be between eighteen and thirty-two.

We were a weakened nation. Food had been abominable, nobody had heard of vitamin pills for chemistry was far behind the chemistry of the Second World War, and we had starved because it was patriotic. The bread was vile, and milk difficult to get for the feeding of stock demanded too much. The gristly sausage, full of anything but pig, might have proved itself to be the backbone of the hungry nation, but the backbone had little marrow in it.

The first incident which brought home the realization that something strange was happening came when I walked into a local shop and bought some ribbon from a young assistant there. As I found that I had insufficient I went again in the afternoon. A small apprentice looked at me with pink eyes; the girl who had served me in the morning had collapsed behind the counter soon after I had left, and she was dead.

'But she can't be!' I gasped. 'Was it heart?'

'Oh no,' said the little apprentice, 'not heart at all, just the influenza.'

Frankly I did not believe that this could happen. I did not realize that this particular 'flu bug developed into a malignant pneumonia at lightning speed. It was a killer which had become violently active in our midst, and the doctors could only use the remedies they had to hand, ones which were already dying of senility.

People continued to die, and so terribly quickly, and all of them were the young. It would almost seem as though it had some association with the great plague of London, yet of course that could not be.

The epidemic accrued at a mighty speed.

Every time I went out more windows had their ragged blinds drawn, ragged from the war and the fact that this last year all thought of repairs had had to go by the board.

My Venetian blinds hung in limp slats bunched together where the binding had given way; the webbing had gone off the market, and had we been able to buy it there was no one left who could have put it on to the tattered blinds for us. Yet houses drew their shabby blinds out of respect for the dead who lay behind their doors, for the Victorian era was still with us in homage to death, in deep mourning, and in respect.

It was the baby's little nursemaid 'Woolly' who contracted it first. She ran a high temperature and I took the baby's cot into my room; by morning the cook had developed it. Mrs. Fanthorpe had a weak heart, something which had always worried us, and the doctor took a serious view of her condition.

He stood in the hall fingering his hat. 'This is a most unpleasant form of influenza,' he said. 'It runs through a house and there is nothing that we can do to stop it.'

I asked if we all should get it, and he said seeing our ages he thought we should, for apparently it hit at the young. When we said goodbye on the step, with the melancholy autumnal garden beyond, he apologized for being so depressed. He had been up all night, and had seen four young people die during that night, two of whom he had brought into the world.

'I have the feeling that this wretched thing never goes through a house without leaving a corpse behind it,' he said.

I wished we had not talked. Arthur on the other hand did not care, he thought that the doctor was a fool anyway, and did not believe a word he said. Arthur had always been casual over death; it did not frighten him; I remembered the time when he and Captain Saw had been holding Holland Gat under the 'No Retreat' order, and how indifferent he had been. His idea was that as we all had to die some time, what was the good of bothering?

The district nurse was a great help, but as she was wanted everywhere she herself was distracted.

If on October the fourth Germany proposed an armistice, we hardly noticed that this even happened. It seemed amazing that we had waited for this moment for four agonizing years, yet when it came we had got past concerning ourselves with it, for the epidemic was increasing at such a speed that we could think of nothing else.

Next to the doctors the parish grave-digger was the hardest-worked man in the place. Whenever I passed the churchyard, at this time of year misty with autumn, and full of the withering lime leaves, I could see one burial service finishing whilst another funeral waited patiently to begin.

I had the 'flu slightly, and was so busy nursing the cook that I did not even go to bed. Indeed, I must have been stronger than I thought. Arthur became ill. His temperature stayed low, far lower than Mrs. Fanthorpe's or Woolly's, had done, but he was desperately restless. When the doctor came next day I hoped that he would say that Arthur's was just a bad cold, but he didn't. He recognized something that I had missed.

'But it certainly isn't a serious condition yet,' he told me.

From that moment things became difficult.

I and the parlourmaid were the only two left, and because Woolly was ill wherever I went I had to carry the baby with me. He was a heavy child, almost a year old, and although a very amenable baby his weight tired me out.

All through that day restlessness disturbed Arthur; it was midnight when he started a haemorrhage. The doctor came but had to leave later, and when I returned from seeing him out, Arthur was violently delirious. We could get no nurses, the military police came for short shifts, and an old man once an orderly at Netley Hospital. I stayed with Arthur lest the strangers made him afraid.

At the end of three days I think I had forgotten how one slept. My mother-in-law refused to take any message though in the end I got the doctor to speak to her. That night a large stout nurse came down to us. She was a nice woman, only too anxious to help. Arthur lay unconscious in one room, the cook frailly convalescent in another, Woolly just able to sit up in bed, whilst I could recognize a rapidly approaching breakdown in myself, for the dress which had fitted me last week hung now in folds.

In the end Hermon arrived. He walked into the house one dreary morning when I was at the end of my tether and dizzy for the want of sleep. I saw him coming in at the gate where the 'red-hot pokers' dripped dew in the border, against their spiky white leaves which the frost had shattered.

'The war's ending, it may even be over now,' said Hermon.

He was terribly good to me; very kind. He gave me brandy, and for the first time in my life I did not recoil from it, for the simple reason that I hardly tasted it.

That night Arthur died.

After the funeral I went with Hermon to Norwich to stay for a week. He thought it would be better for me than staying on here where everything had happened. They lived in lodgings, so I had to have a room out, and it was one of those poverty-stricken rooms of my childhood, with thready carpets and draughts everywhere. I had to lay my clothes on my dressing-case when I went to bed, for there was no chair. I had a desperate longing for comfort and there was no comfort here, but it had been kind of Hermon to bring me away, and perhaps I was better in Norwich than I should have been at home.

Hermon told me that Austria had accepted the unconditional peace, that the Kaiser had abdicated and had fled, nobody knew where. Peace was coming.

I got up next day feeling very ill indeed. The papers said that ten millions had died in this war and probably another twenty millions had died through the events the war had caused.

I dressed slowly, somehow fatigue and general collapse had made me ridiculously slow. I wore a black dress, with widow's bands at the wrist, and the bonnet with weeds which my mother-in-law had said was the right thing. She had not communicated with me since Arthur had died, but the old butler had come down to the funeral, and had been kindness itself.

I walked out into the street that chilly November day in Norwich. A soldier's funeral was coming down the road, with a Union Jack flung over the shallow coffin, as once a Jack had been flung across a cart trundling up the High Street at Walton to a similar destination.

Could that have been only four years ago?

At that moment a maroon exploded somewhere in the city.

Oh, not another air-raid! I gasped to myself. It could be nothing else, surely?

I never knew that it was the armistice.

I went back to the wretched lodgings because I had nowhere to go, and I was unutterably alone. The paper had the headlines:

GERMANY SURRENDERS

ALLIES TO ACCEPT THE RHINELAND

FLEET GIVEN UP OR DISARMED

The leading article was headed, 'A Glorious End', and under it was the couplet:

What have we gained? The whole world's praise,
Friendship and trust, as it stands at gaze.

It was over; or wasn't it?

THE END

ABOUT THE AUTHOR

Ursula Bloom was one of the most popular bestselling authors of the twentieth century. She wrote over 560 books, a feat which earned her a place in the Guinness Book of World Records for many years, as the world's most prolific female writer. She also wrote short stories, radio and stage plays, and worked as a Fleet Street journalist.

During her long career, as well as writing books under her own name, Ursula used the pen names Sheila Burns, Lozania Prole, Rachel Harvey, Mary Essex and Deborah Mann.

You can read more great stories by Ursula Bloom, and find out more about her life, by visiting her official website www.ursulabloom.com

14183319R00125

Printed in Great Britain
by Amazon